Indigenous Rights in One Minute

Also by Bruce McIvor

Standoff: Why Reconciliation Fails ·
 Indigenous People and How to Fix It

Bruce McIvor

INDIGENOUS RIGHTS
in One Minute

*What You Need to Know
to Talk Reconciliation*

NIGHTWOOD EDITIONS

2025

Nightwood Editions

P.O. Box 1779

Gibsons, BC VON 1VO

Canada

www.nightwoodeditions.com

COVER DESIGN: Topshelf Creative in collaboration with Bracken Hanuse Corlett
(Wuikinuxv and Klahoose Nations)

TYPOGRAPHY: Rafael Chimicatti

PROOFREAD: Rebecca Hendry

Nightwood Editions acknowledges the support of the Canada Council for the Arts, the Government of Canada, and the Province of British Columbia through the BC Arts Council.

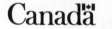

This book has been printed on 100% post-consumer recycled paper.

Printed and bound in Canada.

LIBRARY AND ARCHIVES CANADA CATALOGUING IN PUBLICATION

Title: Indigenous rights in one minute : what you need to know to talk reconciliation / Bruce McIvor.

Names: McIvor, Bruce, author

Description: Includes index.

Identifiers: Canadiana (print) 20250158817 | Canadiana (ebook) 20250158833 |
ISBN 9780889714885 (softcover) | ISBN 9780889714892 (EPUB)

Subjects: LCSH: Indigenous peoples—Legal status, laws, etc.—Canada—Popular works. |
LCSH: Indigenous peoples—Civil rights—Canada—Popular works. |
LCSH: Indigenous peoples—Canada—Government relations—Popular works. |
CSH: Indigenous title—Canada—Popular works. | LCGFT: Law for laypersons.

Classification: LCC KE7709 .M35 2025 | LCC KF8205 M35 2025 kfmod | DDC 342.7108/72—dc23

For my clients

Contents

SECTION II
The Top 50 Aboriginal Law Decisions and Why They Are Important

Preface

This book is not intended for lawyers. It's meant for non-lawyers interested in Canada's commitment to reconciliation with Indigenous Peoples, and how to make it a reality. I have done my best to ensure the entries are accurate, but have no pretensions of being impartial. There will be lawyers, academics and judges who disagree with my editorial comments—fair enough.

The fact that informed, reasonable people have different perspectives on what court decisions mean, as well as those decisions' shortcomings and strengths, underscores the important point that law is not an absolute truth that only judges may generously explain to the rest of us.

The law is alive and constantly changing—sometimes subtly, sometimes unexpectedly quickly. It has a history. It reflects the biases, prejudices and particular worldviews of the judges who make it—many of whom have long ago made the journey to the place of no return. The law expresses society's vision and its shortsightedness, its generosity and its meanness, its fears and its hopes for a better future.

Members of the legal profession are responsible for not only explaining and demystifying the law to improve access to justice, but just as importantly, for holding lawyers, judges, politicians and government officials to account, so that the law, both in its application and its evolution, supports the bringing into existence of a better tomorrow for Indigenous people in Canada. To the best of my abilities, this book is a small contribution to that honourable undertaking.

Aboriginal law (not to be confused with Indigenous law—see page 32) is a wide and ever-growing area of Canadian law. This book does not attempt to cover it all. If you're looking for details about the law surrounding the Indian Act, such as elections and registration, you won't find the answers here. Instead, this book seeks to explain the law on the constitutional protection for Aboriginal rights and treaty rights, against federal and provincial interference with these rights.

The book is divided into two sections. The first includes short, readable answers to the questions I'm most often asked about Indigenous rights. The questions come from my nearly thirty years of working for First Nations, the courses I've taught at the Peter A. Allard School of Law at the University of British Columbia and the Haida Gwaii Institute, and the dozens of workshops I've conducted for First Nations and non-Indigenous organizations across Canada. The format is one-sentence answers followed by longer explanations. I've done my best to limit each explanation to what most people can read in a minute. The second section follows a similar format. It includes concise explanations—from my perspective—of the leading court decisions in Aboriginal law and why they are important.

Understanding the role of Canadian law in colonization starts with understanding the language it uses. Some of the terminology in this book will be jarring for many readers, e.g. "Who is an Indian?" I use these words, including "Aboriginal," in their legal context, not because I accept or endorse them as acceptable categories or descriptors. "Indigenous People" is another way to refer to an Indigenous Nation. "Indigenous people" refers to individuals. Keywords are set in boldface and definitions can be found in the Glossary at the back of the book.

Whether you're completely new to Indigenous rights, have a basic understanding, want a refresher on key principles or are hoping to win an argument with a friend, family member or co-worker, I hope you find *Indigenous Rights in One Minute* useful and informative. Most of all, I hope you find it simple and easy to read.

Bruce McIvor
Vancouver
January 2025

SECTION I

The Most Important Questions About Indigenous Rights

BASICS

Why Do Indigenous People Have Special Rights?

Indigenous People have special rights under Canadian law because their ancestors had distinct legal traditions and rights in their lands before Europeans began to colonize what we now call Canada.

While ancestry is an integral part of Indigenous identity, Indigenous Peoples' rights are not "race-based." Indigenous people have special rights because they are part of a distinct Indigenous Nation with its own language, culture, political and legal systems and its own land base. Importantly, each distinct Indigenous Nation pre-dates the arrival of colonizing European nations (for an explanation of Métis rights see page 38). Indigenous Peoples' rights were not bestowed on them.

Some Indigenous Nations entered into treaties with Britain and later Canada. As part of a treaty, the Crown agreed to honour and respect the Indigenous Nation's pre-existing rights. Later, section 35(1) of the Constitution Act, 1982 provided constitutional protection to these treaty rights and other rights, but it is not the source of these rights.

What Is Section 35?

Section 35 provides constitutional protection for the Aboriginal and treaty rights of the Aboriginal Peoples of Canada.

Section 35 came into effect on April 17, 1982, as part of the Constitution Act, 1982. Its protection applies to Aboriginal and treaty rights existing as of that date. In subsequent court cases, the Crown often argued that an Aboriginal or treaty right had been extinguished before April 17, 1982. Section 35 did not create new rights and is not the source of Aboriginal and treaty rights. These rights existed under Canadian law before section 35. Section 35 is not part of the Charter of Rights and Freedoms.

There was an intention to hold a subsequent constitutional conference in the 1980s to identify and define the rights protected by section 35. Because this never happened, this task has been left up to the courts. The Supreme Court's first major step in interpreting section 35 was the 1990 *Sparrow* decision. The Court decided the fundamental purpose of section 35 is to protect the distinctiveness of the Aboriginal Peoples of Canada and ensure they continue to exist into the future. In the 1996 *Van der Peet* decision, the Court set out the test for defining Aboriginal rights protected by section 35.

From the outset, the Court emphasized that the rights protected under section 35 are not absolute. In *Sparrow* and the 1996 *Badger* decisions, it explained how the Crown can justify interfering with these rights. If the Crown cannot justify a law's interference with an Aboriginal or treaty right protected by section 35, the courts will declare the law invalid to the extent that it interferes with the right. This is because Canada is a **constitutional democracy**. All laws must comply with the constitution. In this way, the rights of Indigenous Peoples in Canada are in a very different legal position than the rights of Indigenous Peoples in other settler-colonial countries such as Australia, New Zealand and the United States, which do not have similar constitutional protection.

What Is the Crown?

The Crown is the embodiment of government authority and obligations.

In the context of Aboriginal law, a reference to the Crown is usually shorthand for either a federal or provincial government's authority under the constitution and their obligations to Indigenous people.

The Crown's authority has two sources: its inherent powers, and the powers granted it by Parliament or a provincial legislature through enactment of a law.

The Crown's inherent powers are the powers that traditionally were exercised by the King or Queen, for example the power to enter into a treaty with another country. These powers are called the "royal prerogative," i.e. the Crown's exclusive rights or powers. In Canada the royal prerogative still exists, but it is much more limited than it was under the British kings and queens of old. The Crown's royal prerogative is exercised by decisions of the government executive, i.e. cabinet.

The second source for the Crown's authority is either Parliament or a provincial legislature. Both can pass laws authorizing cabinet to take a specific action or make a decision.

An independent tribunal, such as the British Columbia Utilities Commission, can become "the Crown" when a law authorizes it to exercise executive powers usually reserved for cabinet. A federal or provincial law often authorizes a government official to make a decision, e.g. the chief forester might be authorized to approve a forestry plan. When this happens, the government official becomes "the Crown." Government-owned companies can also be the Crown. This often happens when they are designated as a "Crown agent" by a federal or provincial law, such as most provincial hydroelectric companies.

What Is the Doctrine of Discovery?

The Doctrine of Discovery is a legal principle that claims European countries extinguished Indigenous sovereignty and acquired the underlying title to Indigenous Peoples' lands upon "discovering" them.

The **Doctrine of Discovery** is inspired by racist fifteenth-century papal bulls dividing up "uncivilized" Indigenous lands for European colonizing countries. It became a legal principle through United States Supreme Court decisions of the 1820s and 1830s. It made its way into Canadian law in the 1880s through the *St. Catherine's Milling* decision. The doctrine has been repudiated around the world. Nonetheless, the dubious and racist legal principles that underlay the Doctrine of Discovery are fundamental to the Supreme Court of Canada's interpretation of section 35. The often-used phrase assertion of Crown sovereignty is a Canadian euphemism for the Doctrine of Discovery.

The continued centrality of the Doctrine of Discovery to modern Canadian Aboriginal law is the source of many Indigenous people's rejection of the Canadian legal system and government policies on "reconciliation."

What Is the Assertion of Crown Sovereignty?

The assertion of Crown sovereignty was a political act by which the British Crown asserted ultimate law-making authority over Indigenous lands and Indigenous people.

The **assertion of Crown sovereignty** over what is now Canada took place at different times and in different forms. For example, the British asserted sovereignty over much of eastern North America through the Royal Proclamation of 1763 following its defeat of France in the Seven Years' War.

On the West Coast, the courts have identified the Treaty of Oregon of 1846, which established the southwestern boundary between British North America and the United States, as the date of the assertion of Crown sovereignty.

The assertion of Crown sovereignty is about who has supreme law-making authority, not whether the Crown owns the land. Unfortunately, this distinction is often lost on politicians and, in some cases, the courts. To the frustration of Indigenous people, Canadian courts have consistently insisted they lack jurisdiction to question the legality of the assertion of Crown sovereignty.

What Is the Royal Proclamation of 1763?

The Royal Proclamation of 1763 represents fundamental principles that continue to inform the legal relationship between Indigenous and non-Indigenous people, including the recognition of Indigenous Peoples' inherent rights and that only the Crown can negotiate for Indigenous lands.

The **Royal Proclamation of 1763** was proclaimed by King George III shortly after the end of the Seven Years' War between France and Great Britain in North America and Britain's acquisition of New France. It drew a north-south line between the American colonies and lands to the west reserved for Indigenous people. This line was one of the points of disagreement that led to the American Revolution in 1776.

While not a source of Indigenous rights, the proclamation has long been recognized by Indigenous people and the courts as an early recognition by the Crown of Indigenous rights. The proclamation established the principle that local colonial, settler governments could not take or sell Indigenous land.

The proclamation also represents the Crown's unilateral assertion of sovereignty over Indigenous people and their land. To be properly understood, the Royal Proclamation must be considered together with the Treaty of Niagara of 1764.

How Does Law-making Work in Canada?

The Crown's law-making authority is primarily confined to the federal parliament and provincial legislatures.

In Canada, law-making is distributed under the constitution between the federal government and the provincial governments. This is what makes Canada a federation, just as the United States and Australia are federations. It means that Indigenous people are potentially subject to laws passed by either the federal government or the provincial governments.

Parliament and the provincial legislatures have the power to make any law and abolish any existing law as long as they stick to the subject matters allocated to them under the constitution. This is referred to as the principle of **parliamentary sovereignty**. There are limitations on parliamentary sovereignty. One of them is that since they were protected under the constitution in 1982, a law cannot extinguish Aboriginal and treaty rights.

The courts decide whether either Parliament or a province has trespassed on the other's law-making authority. In reality, it is usually the provinces who complain that a federal law has overstepped. In Canadian law, the legal issue as to whether the federal or provincial governments can pass a law on any particular topic is called "the division of powers."

Both Parliament and provincial legislatures can pass a law empowering another entity to make laws. The provinces assign certain law-making powers to municipalities, e.g. zoning and property taxes. The federal government delegates limited law-making powers to First Nation Chiefs and Councils through the Indian Act, e.g. regulating traffic on reserve lands. Importantly, this doesn't constitute a recognition of the inherent law-making authority of municipalities or Indian Act bands. Instead, these are examples of delegated powers.

One of the most pressing issues in Canadian law is Indigenous Peoples' inherent law-making authority. Assuming it's recognized, how is this authority recognized and enforced under Canadian law? For more on this issue see the summaries of the *Campbell* and the *C-92 Reference* decisions.

Why Is the Division of Powers Important?

The division of powers is important because it essentializes Indigenous people and disregards their inherent rights and law-making authority.

The Crown's law-making powers are divided between the federal and provincial governments. Section 91 of the constitution lists the topics the federal government has exclusive authority over. Section 92 lists the topics the provincial governments have exclusive authority over. Provincial topics include the management and sale of public lands, municipalities, hospitals, etc. Federal topics include the postal service, the military, currency, banking, etc.

The federal government's side of the ledger includes, at section 24, "Indians, and lands reserved for the Indians." In Canadian Aboriginal law, this is referred to as **section 91(24)**. Historically, it has had a greater effect on Indigenous people than the better-known section 35, which protects Aboriginal and treaty rights.

The principle that the central, overarching government, e.g. the federal government, should have responsibility and control over Indigenous people and their land dates back to the Royal Proclamation of 1763. One reason for the principle was the concern that Indigenous people should be protected by the central government from local settlers. The other was that the central government's control over Indigenous people and their lands would facilitate the wider colonization project. These two reasons were behind assigning the federal government law-making power over Indigenous people and their lands when the Dominion of Canada was created in 1867.

Sections 91 and 92 are not water-tight compartments. The Supreme Court has developed elaborate principles and tests for determining whether a law passed by one level of government intrudes on the "exclusive" powers of the other level of government. For section 91(24), the question becomes whether a provincial law directly affects the "core" of what it means to be an "Indian." Consequently, provincial motor vehicle laws apply on reserves because driving isn't considered to be at the core of being an "Indian," but provincial matrimonial property laws don't apply because control of property is seen as being part of the core of being an Indian.

The thinking behind section 91(24) is important because it influenced the Supreme Court when it considered the purpose for the protection of Aboriginal and treaty rights under section 35. Instead of accepting that section 35 was intended to protect Indigenous people as self-governing nations with their own laws, the Court decided section 35, similar to section 91(24), is about protecting the essential core of what it is to be an "Indian."

Who Is an Indian?

Under Canadian law the word "Indian" is used for different categories of people, including those who are status, non-status, section 35 Indians and section 91(24) Indians.

In Canadian law, the use of the word "Indian" to refer to members of an Indigenous Nation or tribe dates back to the Royal Proclamation of 1763. The Canadian constitution uses the word "Indian," both in the 1867 and the 1982 versions. Up until recently, Indian or Native was the term most often used in Canadian law for a member of an Indigenous Nation. This has gradually been replaced by First Nations or First Nation person.

Status Indians: An Indian can mean a person registered or entitled to be registered under the Indian Act. All status Indians are also section 91(24) Indians. The vast majority, but not necessarily all status Indians are also section 35 Indians. Some status Indians would not qualify as citizens of Indigenous Nations based on an Indigenous Nation's citizenship laws.

Non-status Indians: An Indian can mean a person who identifies as a member of an Indigenous Nation but is not entitled to be registered under the Indian Act. With changes to the registration provisions of the Indian Act, many non-status Indians have become status Indians. Most non-status Indians are section 91(24) Indians. Most, but not necessarily all, non-status Indians are also section 35 Indians.

Section 35 Indians: Section 35 Indians are people entitled to exercise Aboriginal rights under section 35 of the constitution because they are a member of one of the Aboriginal Peoples of Canada. Status Indians are presumed to be section 35 Indians although there are likely status Indians who are not section 35 Indians because they are not part of one of the Aboriginal Peoples of Canada. A person does not have to be a Canadian citizen or a resident of Canada to be a section 35 Indian (see "Why Is the *Desautel* Decision Important?").

Section 91(24) Indians: Section 91(24) of the constitution assigns legislative responsibility for "Indians" to the federal government (see

"Why Is the *Daniels* Decision Important?"). This category includes status Indians, non-status Indians, Métis and Inuit. As between federal and provincial governments, the federal government has exclusive authority to pass laws directly affecting these people, e.g the Indian Act. A person can be a section 91(24) Indian, but not be an Indian under the Indian Act or an Indian under section 35 of the constitution. They might not be entitled to exercise section 35 Aboriginal rights.

The above legal categories are the creation of Canada's legal system. Indigenous people self-identify based on their own laws and traditions. Many identify based on membership in their particular Indigenous Nation and community. Many prefer "First Nation" over "Indigenous" because it avoids the use of the word "Indian," but also differentiates them from the Métis.

What Is a First Nation?

The term First Nation is used in different contexts to describe a group of Indigenous people who, under the Canadian constitution, are called Indians.

Depending on the situation, First Nation might refer to an Indigenous Nation, one of the Aboriginal Peoples of Canada or an Indian Act band.

Indigenous Nation: The term "First Nation" is often used to refer to an Indigenous, self-governing nation that pre-dated the arrival of European colonizers. In this sense, it is equivalent to the term "Nations or Tribes of Indians" used by the British in the Royal Proclamation of 1763.

Aboriginal People of Canada: First Nation is also used to describe one of the "Aboriginal peoples of Canada" whose collective rights are protected under section 35 of the constitution. "Peoples" in section 35 doesn't refer to individuals. It refers to a group or collective of Indigenous people, i.e. a nation. An "Aboriginal people of Canada" is similar to, but not necessarily identical to, an Indigenous Nation because it's a term defined by Canadian law and Canadian courts instead of an Indigenous Nation's own laws and traditions.

Indian Act bands: Confusion arises when First Nation is used to refer to an Indian Act band. Most of today's Indian Act bands were part of larger self-governing Indigenous Nations before the arrival of Europeans. Some local communities or "bands" entered into treaties with the Crown.

The federal government reorganized many of these local communities or bands into Indian Act bands and imposed a new legal definition on them. Under the Indian Act, a band is a group of status Indians with reserve land or entitled to an annuity, e.g. an annual treaty payment. Some local communities or bands were not designated as Indian Act bands and did not enter into treaties with the Crown—these communities continue to fight for recognition.

The federal government has created, terminated, disbanded and forced the amalgamation of Indian Act bands across the country—often as a cost-saving measure or so their reserve lands could be exploited by colonizers (many of whom were federal government employees). The federal government can also create new Indian Act bands.

Some Indian Act bands refuse to adopt the name "First Nation" because they believe it is important to recognize they operate under the thumb of the federal government through the imposition of the Indian Act and that they are part of a larger sovereign Indigenous Nation not subject to definition or control by the federal government.

Who Qualifies as Métis?

To be Métis under section 35 of the constitution, a person must self-identify as Métis, have an ancestral connection to a historic Métis community and be accepted by a modern-day Métis community descended from the historic community.

There is a lot of confusion about being Métis. Many people think self-identifying as Métis and having an Indigenous ancestor, no matter how ancient, qualifies them as being Métis under section 35 of the constitution. They are wrong.

Self-identification and having an Indigenous ancestor is not enough. To be considered Métis for the purpose of exercising rights under section 35, a person must have an ancestral connection to a specific historic Métis community. The historic community must have had a collective identity and shared a common way of life.

The historic Métis community needs to have been in existence when the Crown began to impose its laws in that particular area. The person claiming to be Métis must demonstrate their ancestors were part of that particular historic community. The final requirement is proof of acceptance by the modern-day Métis community that is the successor of the historic community.

Many people, innocently or not, claim to be Métis based on self-identification, having an Indigenous ancestor and membership in a Métis organization. They fail to understand that to claim Métis section 35 rights, they also need to demonstrate an ancestral connection to a specific historic Métis community. Membership in a province-wide so-called "Métis Nation" is not sufficient for meeting the *Powley* test.

Indigenous identity fraud thrives on ignorance and misinformation. It injures and silences Métis uninterested in benefits and entitlements, Métis whose sole motivation is honouring their ancestors and educating their children.

Why Don't Indians Pay Taxes?

Indians pay taxes, lots of taxes.

The lie that Indians don't pay taxes is a tool used to oppress and marginalize Indigenous people. The fact that it's commonplace across the country illustrates the continued acceptability of racist stereotypes.

Many Indigenous people with historical treaties understand that their ancestors never agreed to be taxed. But even when the Crown's negotiators reported that they promised Indigenous people a treaty would not lead to the imposition of any tax, the courts have bent over backwards to devise arguments to deny the exemption, such as in the *Benoit* decision about Treaty 8 in 2003.

The common misconception that Indians don't pay taxes stems from a misunderstanding of the Indian Act tax exemption for personal property situated on Indian Act reserves. The exemption exists because duly elected members of Parliament decided it should. They have also decided other members of Canadian society should, in certain cases, be exempt from income tax, including disabled members of the RCMP and Canadian Forces members and veterans. Why criticize one exemption but not the other?

The rationale for the Indian Act tax exemption dates back to the Royal Proclamation of 1763 and the Crown's promise to protect Indigenous land and property from local colonizers and their "settler" governments. Importantly, the exemption is extremely limited. It's only available to Indigenous people who meet the requirements to be registered as an Indian under the Indian Act. Also, their income must be "connected" to a reserve, as determined by the Supreme Court of Canada in the *Dubé* and *Bastien* decisions. If they don't live and work on reserve, they might not qualify. The majority of Indigenous people can't conform to these restrictions and so pay income tax on their income along with most other Canadians.

RIGHTS·

What Is the Difference Between Aboriginal Rights and Indigenous Rights?

Indigenous rights are inherent rights derived from being a member of an Indigenous Nation; Aboriginal rights are practices or activities Canadian courts have decided are integral to what makes Indigenous people uniquely "Aboriginal."

Aboriginal rights are not Indigenous rights. Aboriginal rights are a creation of the colonizer's legal system based on their laws. They are difficult to prove and limited in scope. Inherent rights are the rights of Indigenous people based on their particular nation's laws.

Section 35 of the constitution is not the source of Aboriginal rights. Aboriginal rights were part of Canadian law long before section 35 of the Constitution Act. The existence of Aboriginal rights in Canadian law is based on the fact that before colonizers arrived, Indigenous Peoples were already present, occupying their lands (see "Why Is the *Calder* Decision Important?"). The effect of section 35 was to provide constitutional protection to Aboriginal rights in existence when the constitution came into effect in April 1982.

In 1982 the intention was to hold a subsequent conference to decide what Aboriginal rights were protected by section 35. Because this never happened, it was left to the Supreme Court to decide the purpose of section 35 and how to identify Aboriginal rights. The Court decided Aboriginal rights are based on Indigenous practices essential in making people "Aboriginal" and uncontaminated by European influences (see "Why Is the *Sparrow* Decision Important?" and "Why Is the *Van der Peet* Decision Important?").

Aboriginal rights are not part of the Charter of Rights and Freedoms and so are not subject to the notwithstanding clause. The charter protects individual rights from interference by government, e.g. freedom of speech. Section 35 Aboriginal rights protect the communal rights of "Aboriginal people."

Aboriginal rights in existence in 1982 cannot be formally extinguished by federal or provincial governments. But, the Court decided Aboriginal rights are not absolute—they can be infringed by the Crown for a wide range of purposes (see "Why Is the *Delgamuukw* Decision Important?"). The constitutional protection against extinguishment is not as reassuring as many would assume because for all intents and purposes infringement can equal extinguishment.

Who Is Entitled to Benefit from Aboriginal and Treaty Rights?

Determining who is entitled to benefit from Aboriginal and treaty rights requires identifying the "Aboriginal people" under section 35.

Aboriginal rights and treaty rights are communal rights, i.e. they are held by an "Aboriginal people of Canada" which is a group, collective or society of "Indians." Determining who is entitled to benefit from section 35 rights requires first identifying the "Aboriginal people," i.e. what is the group or collective and, second, identifying the members of that group or collective.

For First Nations with historical treaties, identifying the group or collective starts with determining the group that agreed to a treaty with the Crown. Subject to the federal government's reorganization of Indian Act bands, in most cases there is a modern-day Indian Act band that corresponds to the group that agreed to the treaty.

For **non-treaty First Nations**, it's more complicated. Under Canadian law, an Indian Act band is not necessarily equivalent to an "Aboriginal people" under section 35 of the constitution. The makeup of an "Aboriginal people" for the purposes of exercising Aboriginal rights is determined from the perspective of the Indigenous people themselves based on their shared history, language and culture (see *Tsilhqot'in* at the BC Court of Appeal in "What Is Required to Prove Aboriginal Title?"). Many modern-day Indigenous Nations or "Aboriginal people" consider themselves to be made up of several Indian Act bands.

Identifying the members of the collective is not straightforward. It is usually assumed that a status Indian on an Indian Act band list is a member of one of the "Aboriginal people" of Canada under section 35, but this is not necessarily correct. A small number of people are status

Indians based on the federal government's requirements for registration and are placed on an Indian Act band list by the federal government but are not recognized as members of the collective based on Indigenous people's own laws and traditions.

Similarly, there is a large number of **non-status Indians** who don't qualify to register under the Indian Act but are members of one of the "Aboriginal people" of Canada under section 35 based on Indigenous People's laws and traditions.

As an outcome of court decisions, the federal government has repeatedly changed the registration criteria under the Indian Act to remove restrictions on registration. For example, in the 1980s Bill C-31 addressed the injustice of Indian women losing their status when they married a non-Indian man. As a result, tens of thousands of women regained their status. Becoming a status Indian didn't mean these women were newly entitled to benefit from their First Nation's section 35 rights—they always were entitled.

An increasing number of Indigenous Nations recognize that accepting Indian Act registration as the means of identifying their members is fraught with inequity. It disentitles many of the nation's members, including cousins, nephews, nieces and grandchildren because they can't meet the requirements for Indian Act registration. It also endangers their future because depending on who they marry, a member's children might not be entitled to be a status Indian. In response, they identify their members by developing citizenship laws based on their own traditions.

How Do Courts Limit the Impact of Aboriginal Rights?

Canadian courts limit the impact of Aboriginal rights by exercising their power to recharacterize the rights claimed by Indigenous people.

Under Canadian law, section 35 Aboriginal rights are not property rights, i.e. they aren't about owning anything (for Aboriginal title and property rights see "What Is Aboriginal Title?"). Instead, they are rights to do certain things that, from the courts' perspective, make Indigenous people "Aboriginal."

To limit section 35 in this way, the Supreme Court decided Aboriginal rights are based on pre-contact Indigenous practices integral to the distinctive culture of the Indigenous people claiming the right.

The courts routinely reject Indigenous people's description of their Aboriginal rights and substitute a narrower, more specific description (see "Why Is the *Mitchell* Decision Important?" and "Why Is the *Pamajewon* Decision Important?"). The result is that Indigenous people fail in court because they present evidence for an Aboriginal right and then are told they actually needed to present evidence for a different right. It's as if someone presents evidence they saw a chicken only to be later told they needed to prove they saw a specific type of chicken, a Rhode Island Red.

Even if an Aboriginal right claim survives the courts' redefining of the right, the end result can be a right with limited practical utility. For example, in the *Sappier* decision of 2006, the Mi'kmaq and Wolastoqiyik claimed a right to harvest timber for personal uses. The Supreme Court decided that description was too general and that the right had to focus on how, pre-contact, the Mi'kmaq and Wolastoqiyik used wood as part of fishing, hunting and travelling on rivers and lakes. The

Court redefined the right as the right to harvest timber for domestic uses as a member of a Mi'kmaq or Wolastoqiyik community.

Recharacterized in this way, the right has no commercial aspect. Even selling timber to raise money to build a house is, according to the Court, offside. Also, timber can't be harvested for personal use—the harvesting must be done to support the distinctive character of Mi'kmaq and Wolastoqiyik societies.

The *Sappier* decision is an example of Canadian courts using their power to recharacterize claimed Aboriginal rights to reduce the likelihood that Indigenous people will succeed in court and even when they do succeed, to ensure that the resulting right does not pose a threat to non-Indigenous society and its economic interests.

What Is the Basis
for Métis Rights?

Métis rights are based on Métis customs, practices and traditions that emerged between the time of European contact and the date colonizers began to control the land.

For many years there was uncertainty as to the basis for Métis constitutionally protected rights. If Aboriginal rights are derived from Indigenous Peoples' occupation of their lands before colonizers arrived, how could the Métis have rights when they didn't exist before the arrival of Europeans?

In the 2003 *Powley* decision, the Supreme Court created a test for proving Métis rights that allowed for the emergence of Métis rights after the arrival of Europeans. The Court held that Métis rights protected under the constitution are based on Métis customs, practices and traditions that developed after the Métis emerged as a distinct people and prior to the imposition of European laws.

The date of the imposition of the colonizers' laws—the legal term is "the date of effective control"—varies across the country. It is specific to the Métis community claiming an Aboriginal right. For example, in *Powley* the Court held that the date of effective control for the Sault Ste. Marie Métis community was 1850. Farther west, the courts have held that the date of effective control in southeastern Alberta was 1874, while in southwestern Manitoba it would have been 1880.

What Rights Do the Métis Have?

For most Métis, their rights under section 35 of the constitution are more limited than the constitutional rights of First Nations and the Inuit.

Most Métis rights fall into two broad categories: rights confirmed in court and **asserted rights**. There are also Métis treaty rights, but they are the exception. For example, in 1993 the Métis of Fort Good Hope and Fort Norman/Norman Wells in the Northwest Territories, along with the Sahtu Dene, entered into a land claims agreement with Canada. Métis rights under the land claims agreement are treaty rights under section 35 of the constitution.

Métis section 35 rights confirmed by the courts are few and far between. When the Métis have been successful, the courts have confirmed local, site-specific harvesting rights, e.g. a right to hunt for food in the Sault Ste. Marie area and a right to hunt for food in southwestern Manitoba. Attempts to establish region-wide rights have been unsuccessful.

In many cases, Métis rights are asserted, but not proven. All section 35 asserted Aboriginal rights must pass a credibility standard. If government decides the claim is not credible, there is no obligation to consult the Métis. This is the case in British Columbia where the provincial government does not recognize any credible claims of Métis section 35 Aboriginal rights.

If the claim is credible, the next step for government is to determine the required level of consultation based on the strength of claim and potential impact of a government decision on the asserted right. For credible but weak claims, government obligations include notice, information sharing and ensuing discussion.

While the Métis might have a credible claim for harvesting rights in some parts of Canada, any claim for an interest in the land must overcome a significant obstacle. The Supreme Court considered the question of Métis Aboriginal title in *Manitoba Métis* and concluded that because Aboriginal title is a communal right and the Métis regularly bought and sold land as individuals, they likely do not have a claim for Aboriginal title (see "Why Is the *Manitoba Métis* Decision Important?").

The Court's reasoning is significant because any Métis claim to revenue sharing or decision-making over the land must be grounded in a credible Aboriginal title claim. If there is no credible claim, it is unlikely governments have an obligation to consult and accommodate the Métis about their asserted interest in the land.

What Was Métis Scrip?

Métis scrip was a certificate issued by the federal government for either land or money as fulfillment of its promise to set aside 1.4 million acres of land for the children of the Métis.

Following Confederation in 1867, the first major step in Canada's colonization project was its acquisition of the Hudson's Bay Company land interests in western and northern Canada.

When the Canadian government attempted to exercise control of land in the Red River settlement in present-day Manitoba in 1869, the Métis mounted a resistance. This led to the negotiated entry of Manitoba into Confederation in 1870 through the passing of the Manitoba Act. One of the terms of the act was that 1.4 million acres of land would be allocated to Métis heads of families for settling their children. This is referred to as "the children's grant."

Manitoba's entry into Confederation sparked an immediate rush of non-Indigenous people to the new province. While the new government delayed confirming the land allotment for the Métis children, these colonizers began acquiring land.

In the early 1870s, with much of the Métis land grant still unallocated, the government started issuing certificates confirming individual entitlements to either land or money. This is referred to as Métis scrip. Different values of scrip were issued over the years. The value of money scrip ranged up to $240. Land scrip could be for as much as 240 acres but it was difficult to redeem because of the delay in surveying lands and government restrictions on which lands could be selected. Métis scrip was subject to rampant fraud and speculation. As a consequence, many Métis children never received their land grant.

In 1981 the Manitoba Métis Federation filed a lawsuit against Canada for breach of fiduciary duty based on its failure to fulfill its promises under the Manitoba Act. While they lost at trial and the Manitoba Court of Appeal, in 2013 the Supreme Court granted them a declaration that Canada failed to fulfill its promise to the Métis children in accordance with the honour of the Crown (see "Why Is the *Manitoba Métis* Decision Important?"). Ever since, they have been in negotiations to resolve the Crown's failure to fulfill what the Supreme Court described as a constitutional promise to the Métis.

What Is Aboriginal Title?

Aboriginal title is Indigenous Peoples' constitutionally protected right to benefit from their lands and decide how their lands are used.

Aboriginal title, one of the Aboriginal rights protected under section 35 of the constitution, is more than a bundle of harvesting rights: it is a right to the land itself. It includes the right to exclude other people from the land, the right to benefit from the land and the right to make decisions about the land.

The Supreme Court's description of Aboriginal title does not disturb its acceptance of the Doctrine of Discovery. In Canadian law, Aboriginal title is a burden on the Crown's underlying title that was acquired through the simple assertion of Crown sovereignty over Indigenous lands.

The interest in land most people in Canada are familiar with is called fee simple title—this is the title you have to any property you might own. Aboriginal title is not equal to fee simple title. Unlike people and companies who own land in fee simple, Indigenous people cannot use Aboriginal title lands in such a way that would deny future generations the right to use and benefit from the land.

There is an important exception to this rule that favours Canada's ongoing colonization project: one generation of Indigenous people can disentitle future generations by surrendering the Nation's Aboriginal title to the Crown. This is the fundamental objective of Canada's comprehensive claims policy.

The recognition of Aboriginal title does not mean lands are protected from exploitation by provincial and federal governments. Aboriginal title can be infringed, i.e. extinguished, for a number of reasons including forestry, mining, hydroelectricity, building infrastructure and settling foreign populations.

While a powerful tool for protecting Indigenous rights, Aboriginal title is not the same as an Indigenous People's inherent title. Aboriginal title is a creature of Canadian law. It is based on the acceptance of the Doctrine of Discovery and has built-in limits and exceptions to ensure it doesn't become an insurmountable obstacle to removing Indigenous people from their lands so those lands can be exploited by non-Indigenous people.

What Is Required to Prove Aboriginal Title?

To prove their Aboriginal title, Indigenous people must convince a court their ancestors exclusively used and occupied their lands at the time of the assertion of Crown sovereignty.

The 1973 *Calder* decision opened up the possibility of Aboriginal title, but it wasn't until the 1997 *Delgamuukw* decision that the Supreme Court explained what it was and created a test for proving it exists. After years of confusion and uncertainty, the 2014 *Tsilhqot'in* decision clarified the test for Aboriginal title.

The test requires Indigenous people to prove their ancestors had exclusive use and occupation of their lands at the date the Crown asserted sovereignty, i.e. the date the Doctrine of Discovery was applied to their lands. Because colonization occurred over a long time period, this date varies widely across the country.

A 2005 Supreme Court decision (*Marshall* & *Bernard*) created confusion about Aboriginal title because it seemed to indicate that Indigenous people would only be able to prove title to small parts of their territory they used intensively, e.g. salt licks and buffalo jumps. The BC Court of Appeal's decision to follow this rationale in *Tsilhqot'in* (2012) was overturned in 2014 by the Supreme Court of Canada, which clarified that it was possible for Indigenous people to make out Aboriginal title claims on a territorial basis, i.e. it could consist of more than mere dots on a map.

Instead of requiring the Crown to prove how it acquired an interest in Indigenous lands, Canadian courts assume the Crown has a legitimate interest. They then put the onus on Indigenous people to prove an interest in their own land. By accepting the Crown's unproven claim, the courts ensure they don't disrupt the ongoing exploitation of Indigenous land and reward governments who pursue a policy of denying Indigenous Peoples' rights.

Until they prove their title in court or convince a government to recognize it, Indigenous People are left with the **duty to consult** to defend their lands (see "Why Is the Duty to Consult Inadequate?"). If they try to enforce their own Indigenous laws and exercise their Aboriginal title, they are criminalized by the Canadian court system and end up in jail.

What Does "Site-specific" Mean?

"Site-specific" means that for some section 35 rights, Indigenous people are limited to exercising them within a specific tract of land or territory.

The Supreme Court explained the "site-specific" requirement in its 1996 *Adams* and *Côté* decisions. Because section 35 Aboriginal rights are based on pre-contact practices, the exercise of some Aboriginal rights is limited to the geographical area of the Aboriginal practice or activity pre-contact.

As part of efforts to limit their legal obligation to respect Aboriginal rights, governments often misapply the "site-specific" requirement. When fulfilling the duty to consult, they insist Indigenous people produce evidence of precise locations where they exercise their rights, e.g. where exactly they fish, shoot a deer, pick berries, etc. The implication is that as long as the proposed project does not touch on these precise locations—these dots on a map—it can proceed without accommodating the Indigenous Peoples' rights. The Supreme Court never intended such an impoverished approach to Aboriginal rights.

In *Côté*, the Court explained if an Indigenous person relies on an Aboriginal right as a defence to federal or provincial charges, they need to establish that the specific site where they were fishing, shot a deer, etc. was within the wider area over which the right was exercised prior to contact. In *Côté* the geographical area was 100 square kilometres.

In *Adams*, although the fishing in dispute occurred in Lake St. Francis, the Court did not require evidence that the Mohawk had fished in Lake St. Francis. It was sufficient to establish that they had fished in a much wider area, the upper St. Lawrence River valley, which includes Lake St. Francis. Similarly, in *Tsilhqot'in* the Supreme Court rejected the argument that Aboriginal title could only be made out to small, heavily used areas of an Indigenous People's territory.

What Are Comprehensive Claims?

Comprehensive claims are claims by Indigenous Peoples for their own land accepted for negotiation by the federal government.

The federal government announced its comprehensive land claims policy in 1981 in response to the Supreme Court's 1973 *Calder* decision. Up until then, the federal government had denied the existence of Indigenous land rights. While the language has changed over the years, Canada's goal in negotiating comprehensive claims has remained the same—the full and final settlement of Indigenous Peoples' interests in their lands.

Comprehensive land claims are different from specific claims that relate to breaches of treaty and the unlawful use of reserve lands. Specific claims do not involve Aboriginal rights, land outside reserves or governance matters. Comprehensive claims are also different from Aboriginal title claims, which are court actions that seek a declaration of Aboriginal title. First Nations file Aboriginal title claims as part of pursuing recognition and implementation of their Aboriginal title.

If Indigenous Peoples' rights were respected and the Crown's asserted interest in Indigenous land wasn't presumed, it would be the Crown rather than Indigenous Peoples who would be forced into the position of filing land claims. Canada's comprehensive claims policy is part of its longstanding efforts to remove Indigenous people from the land so non-Indigenous people can exploit it. In contrast, Indigenous people are increasingly seeking agreements based on recognition and respect for their inherent and constitutionally protected rights. The 2024 Haida Aboriginal Title recognition agreement demonstrates this is a viable option.

TREATIES

What Are Treaties?

Treaties are an exchange of sacred, solemn promises between the Crown and Indigenous People.

A wide range of treaties have been entered into over the previous 350-plus years between European nations and the Indigenous Peoples of present-day Canada. They include the Peace and Friendship treaties in the seventeenth and eighteenth centuries, the land-centred treaties of the nineteenth and early twentieth centuries and the modern-day, post-*Calder* treaties.

Treaties in Canada have taken diverse forms, ranging from one-paragraph statements to multi-chapter documents filled with legal jargon. They date from the early seventeenth century to the modern-day. Most, but not all, of the judge-made law has focussed on the pre-*Calder* treaties, i.e. "historical treaties." Unless otherwise noted, "treaties" in the following section refers to the law surrounding the pre-*Calder* treaties.

Early treaties, e.g. the Peace and Friendship Treaties of the eighteenth century, were about establishing peaceful trading relations. In the mid-nineteenth century, colonizers began to envision treaties as a tool for gaining control of Indigenous land whereas Indigenous people continued to understand them as sacred agreements establishing peaceful, mutually beneficial relationships. **Treaty First Nations** reject and condemn the argument that their treaties are "surrender" documents.

Canadian courts have emphasized treaties are not simple one-time transactions—they are living documents. The Crown must diligently fulfill treaty promises. In doing so it must act with integrity and avoid sharp dealing.

Many modern treaties claim to modify or extinguish the inherent and pre-existing rights of Indigenous people in exchange for land, money and limited law-making authority. Indigenous people have increasingly rejected this approach to treaty making. Instead of transactional settlements, they seek agreements that recognize and preserve their inherent rights.

What Was Required to Create a Treaty?

A treaty between Indigenous Peoples and the Crown was created when each side intended to create legally binding obligations and their discussions were serious and dignified.

The Crown has a long history of denying the existence of historical treaties with Indigenous Peoples. With the change to the Indian Act in 1951, which removed the ban on First Nations hiring lawyers to defend their rights, Indigenous Peoples went to court to have their treaties recognized.

Their first major victory was the *White and Bob* British Columbia Court of Appeal decision in 1964. It confirmed the 1854 agreement between the Snuneymuxw and Governor Douglas of the Hudson's Bay Company was a treaty and that the treaty rights still existed.

Later Supreme Court of Canada decisions further developed the law. They rejected the argument that the treaties should be interpreted based on the international law of treaties. Instead, the Court developed its own principles based on a broad and liberal interpretation that wasn't overly legalistic and considered the specific historical circumstances.

Over the objections of the Crown, the courts have confirmed the existence of various treaties including the Peace and Friendship Treaty of 1752 between the British and the Mi'kmaq (see "Why Is the *Simon* Decision Important?" and "Why Are the *Marshall* Decisions Important?") and a one-paragraph letter signed by British General Murray in 1760 (shortly after the Battle of Quebec) guaranteeing rights to the Huron-Wendat (see "Why Is the *Sioui* Decision Important?").

Regrettably, even when First Nations win court decisions confirming the existence of their treaties with the Crown, they continue to struggle to have the Crown respect their treaty rights, e.g. Mi'kmaq commercial fishing rights under the Peace and Friendship Treaty of 1752.

How Do the Courts Interpret Treaties?

The courts review the written document and the surrounding evidence to identify the common intention of the parties to the treaty.

Canadian judges long refused to accept there were enforceable treaties between Indigenous Peoples and the Crown. In the infamous 1928 *Syliboy* decision, the Nova Scotia County Court dismissed the 1752 treaty between the Crown and the Mi'kmaq as a "mere agreement" with a handful of "savages." It wasn't until the early 1960s and the *White and Bob* decision from British Columbia that the courts began to recognize historical agreements between Indigenous Peoples and the Crown as treaties.

Having accepted that treaties existed, the courts interpreted them based on technical rules of contract law and focussed obsessively on the words in the document written by the Crown. Eventually, the courts accepted that such a narrow approach was unacceptable. The widely adopted summary of the law on treaty interpretation comes from Justice McLachlin's dissent in the first *Marshall* decision. The overarching principles of interpretation are:

- treaties are special agreements that require special rules of interpretation;
- they should be liberally interpreted and any doubts decided in favour of Indigenous people;
- the goal is to identify the common objective of the parties at the time the treaty was made;
- it is assumed Crown negotiators acted with integrity and honour;
- courts must be alive to the parties' cultural and linguistic differences;
- the words of the treaty must be interpreted based on how they would have been understood at the time the treaty was made;

- the courts should not interpret treaties as technical contracts; and
- while the interpretation should be generous, it must be realistic.

Not all treaty promises were recorded in the Crown's written document. The courts review the evidence surrounding treaty negotiations (written and oral evidence) to identify the oral promises and implied rights that give rise to unwritten treaty rights.

Despite advancements in treaty interpretation, judges still fixate on the written document as being "the treaty." In this way, they privilege the status of the colonizers' self-serving version of the treaty and relegate the surrounding evidence and the Indigenous perspective as mere context useful for interpreting "the treaty." This approach is contrary to legal principles and Indigenous Peoples' understanding of what constitutes the treaty based on their own laws.

Aren't the Treaties with the King?

The courts have decided that although most Indigenous people understand their treaty relationship to be with the British Crown, their treaty partners are the federal and provincial governments.

Dating back to the earliest days of colonization, sovereign Indigenous Nations entered into treaties with European nations. These treaties focussed on trade and military alliances. In the early nineteenth century, British colonizers sought treaties with Indigenous Nations that would give them access to land. Indigenous people understood they were making treaties with the Crown's representatives and by extension with either the Queen or the King.

Canadian courts have gradually whittled away at the relationship between sovereign Indigenous Nations and the King. They began by deciding that instead of viewing the treaties as being between sovereign powers, they should be seen as agreements between the King and his subjects. Therefore, they are not international treaties.

Second, the courts decided that as of Confederation in 1867 the King's responsibilities for treaties transferred to the Canadian federal government as part of its law-making authority over "Indians, and lands reserved for the Indians" under the constitution. First Nations from Alberta, Nova Scotia and New Brunswick challenged this view in the British courts in 1981, as part of a country-wide Indigenous response to the Liberal government's plan to patriate the constitution. The British courts found against them. They decided that although the powers and responsibilities of the Crown had at one time been solely embodied in the King or Queen in England, they had gradually been subdivided across the British Empire and it was now the federal government that represented the Crown for the purposes of fulfilling treaty promises.

In 2014 the Supreme Court took the final step in undermining treaty First Nations' perspective on their treaty relationship by concluding provincial governments could step into the federal government's shoes as the treaty partner and pass laws that interfere with treaty rights (see "Why Is the *Grassy Narrows* Decision Important?").

Didn't First Nations Surrender Their Land Through Treaties?

First Nations did not surrender their land through treaties.

The idea that Indigenous people surrendered their land through historical treaties is, along with the Doctrine of Discovery, one of the fundamental lies that props up Canada's colonization project.

Setting aside the question of whether Indigenous people even had a concept for surrendering their land (which is highly doubtful), anyone with a basic knowledge of early Canadian history knows Europeans continually described the Indigenous People they encountered as sophisticated hard bargainers. They knew the value of things and didn't easily part with their possessions. The idea that the ancestors of today's First Nation members agreed to surrender all their land in exchange for harvesting rights they already had, confinement to reserves and a few additional benefits is absurd.

Indigenous People know this truth. It is a truth passed down to them by their parents and grandparents. In recent years academics researching the question have often agreed with them. But this truth has been slow to take root in Canadian law for three reasons. First, there have been very few trials that directly address the surrender question. When they do occur, trial judges tend to agree with the Indigenous view that they didn't surrender their land.

The second reason the courts continue to perpetuate the falsehood that treaties were surrender documents is that except for the odd trial judge who hears the evidence first-hand, most judges were educated, in school and at home, to accept and perpetuate the fiction that treaties were surrender documents. Like people during the Middle Ages, they inhabit a world where the Earth is at the centre of the universe, waiting for Copernicus to set them straight.

The third reason is that for the courts to seriously question whether historical treaties were surrender documents would be to question the very foundation of the Canadian state. Most judges are unwilling to entertain a question that would lead to a Canadian existential crisis, so the lie is perpetuated and Canada's reconciliation project founders on the rocks of injustice.

Why Are the Natural Resources Transfer Agreements Important?

The Natural Resources Transfer Agreements are important because they represent the Crown's and the courts' lack of respect for the treaty relationship with First Nations.

Under the 1867 constitution, the original four provinces (New Brunswick, Nova Scotia, Ontario and Quebec) were assigned control and ownership of so-called Crown land and resources. When Manitoba was established as a province in 1870 and Alberta and Saskatchewan in 1905, the federal government kept control of Crown land and resources it had purportedly purchased from the Hudson's Bay Company in 1870 because the federal government wanted to control lands in the three prairie provinces as part of Canada's colonization project.

Settlers on Indigenous land in the prairie provinces complained that they were being treated as second-class citizens. Their complaints led to the negotiation in the 1920s of the Natural Resources Transfer Agreements between the federal government and the prairie provinces—three separate but almost identical agreements that transferred control of Crown land and natural resources from the federal to the provincial governments. In 1930 the agreements were given the force of law through a statute passed by the United Kingdom Parliament now referred to as the Constitution Act, 1930.

Between 1870 and the early twentieth century, Indigenous people on the prairies entered into treaties with the Crown—they are part of what are often referred to as the "numbered treaties." Although they were directly affected, treaty First Nations played no part in the negotiations between the federal government and the provinces that led to the Natural Resources Transfer Agreements. The Supreme Court decided the effect of the agreements was to modify and consolidate treaty rights. The agreements, according to the Court, extinguished the treaty right to commercial hunting, allowed the provinces to regulate treaty harvesting rights, but expanded the geographical scope of the rights to the entire province.

The Supreme Court's decisions have been roundly criticized by Indigenous people, lawyers and academics. The Natural Resources Transfer Agreements, and their interpretation by the Supreme Court, remain at the forefront of prairie treaty First Nations' distrust of the Crown and the Canadian court system.

What Rights Are Guaranteed by Treaty?

Treaty rights include written and oral promises, any rights necessary to exercise a treaty right and the right to use modern-day technology.

Governments often take an overly narrow view of treaty rights by focussing on the exact wording in the written document. In so doing, they ignore the courts' treaty interpretation principles and minimize the promises made to Indigenous people.

Treaties between the Crown and First Nations were oral agreements. Identifying treaty rights requires an understanding of what was agreed to by both parties in their face-to-face meetings. The written document does not necessarily represent the oral agreement. It reflects what the Crown may have intended or hoped to achieve as part of the treaty negotiations. It often contains technical terms that either were not explained to First Nations or were most likely not understood in the Western European legal sense as they are understood by modern-day judges. The so-called **"cede, release and surrender"** clauses are a prime example.

Identifying treaty rights requires analyzing the record, written and oral, that explains each side's objectives entering into treaty negotiations. Having identified objectives, it is necessary, as best as possible, to identify the treaty promises made during negotiations. These promises should then be compared to the written document. How do the terms of the written document compare to the promises made or likely made during the oral negotiations? Oral promises may not have been recorded in the written document, nonetheless, they are still enforceable treaty rights. Given that the document was written by and in the language of the Crown, a healthy skepticism should be applied to terms in the written document adverse to the interest of First Nations.

Despite sustained efforts by federal and provincial governments to insist on a narrow interpretation of treaty rights, the courts have repeatedly concluded they are broad and inclusive. For example: hunting rights include the right to travel with a gun and ammunition (see "Why Is the *Simon* Decision Important?"); harvesting rights include the right of access to the harvesting area (see "Why Are the *Adams* and *Côté* Decisions Important?") and the right to build a hunting cabin (see "Why Is the *Sundown* Decision Important?").

Treaty rights are not frozen in time. Although they may have been guaranteed over a hundred years ago, Indigenous people can exercise them today by relying on modern technology. For example, treaties from the 1850s on Vancouver Island guaranteed the right to hunt at night. At the time, Indigenous people hunted at night with torch lamps. In the 2006 *Morris* decision, the Supreme Court confirmed that a modern-day expression of the treaty right includes the use of rifles and high-powered lights.

What Are the Crown's Obligations When It Infringes Treaty Rights?

In many cases, when the Crown infringes treaty rights it must do more than consult with treaty First Nations.

The Crown owes Indigenous people different legal obligations depending on whether it denies or recognizes their rights. When Aboriginal or treaty rights are *denied* (what the courts call "asserted" or "pre-proof" claims), the Crown must consult and, in some situations, accommodate. The Crown retains ultimate decision-making authority and there's no obligation to agree. The duty to consult entitles Indigenous people to a process, not a concrete outcome. This is why it often devolves into notetaking and box-ticking that frustrates Indigenous people.

The Crown's legal obligations are more serious when there are *recognized* treaty rights, including rights guaranteed by the so-called historical treaties, or Aboriginal rights confirmed in court, e.g. the Mi'kmaq commercial fishing right (see "Why Are the *Marshall* Decisions Important?"). In those situations, the Crown often must do more than fulfill its duty to consult. The Crown may have to ensure its proposed project is consistent with its fiduciary relationship with Indigenous people, advances reconciliation, and intrudes on Aboriginal and treaty rights to the smallest possible extent.

Governments often sidestep the more serious legal obligations they owe treaty First Nations by treating them the same as they would non-treaty First Nations with so-called "asserted" Aboriginal rights. They focus on the duty to consult and are silent on the more serious obligations they owe treaty First Nations. While the courts have identified consultation as the requirement when a historical treaty anticipates governments will "take up" land for non-Indigenous exploitation, even then governments must guard against too much land exploitation infringing core treaty promises (see "Why Is the Supreme Court's *Yahey* Decision Important?").

When governments underestimate their obligations to treaty First Nations, they show contempt for the treaty relationship. Based on the Crown's view of what Indigenous people gave up when they entered into treaty, government officials are honour-bound to comply with the full extent of their legal obligations.

What Can First Nations Do About the Provinces' Piecemeal Infringement of Treaty Rights?

Treaty First Nations can insist the provinces have processes in place to monitor the cumulative effects of separate interferences with their treaty rights to ensure they do not combine to undermine fundamental treaty promises.

The written text of many of the so-called historical treaties with First Nations includes a provision that allows the Crown to exploit Indigenous lands for a range of purposes, including mining, forestry, roads, hydroelectricity, pipelines and selling the land to non-Indigenous people. In the law this is described as "taking up" the land and the clause in the treaty is referred to as the "take up" clause.

One "take up" leads to another, which leads to another. Over time, they add up to reduce the land available for First Nations to exercise their treaty rights. This process is referred to as **cumulative effects** or the piecemeal infringement of treaty rights.

Treaty "take up" clauses have been the subject of several important court decisions. In *Mikisew I* in 2005, the Supreme Court decided each individual "take up" of land should not be treated as an infringement of the treaty and for each "take up," First Nations were owed no more than the duty to consult. But, if so much land was eventually taken up that treaty First Nations were left without any meaningful ability to exercise their treaty rights, then this would amount to an infringement of the treaty.

In *Yahey*, the BC Supreme Court decided it would be unconscionable to allow the Crown to continue with the piecemeal infringement
of treaty rights up until the point that treaty rights were as good as
meaningless. Instead, the Crown must monitor the effects of separate,
seemingly unconnected land uses to ensure their cumulative effect
does not break the fundamental promise of the treaty.

Because of the *Yahey* decision, treaty First Nations now have a
strong argument to hold provinces to account for the piecemeal infringement of treaty rights. Whether it be forestry, roads, mines,
pipelines, hydroelectric power or selling off so-called Crown land, the
provinces must demonstrate they have processes in place to monitor
the cumulative effect of piecemeal infringements of treaty rights.

OBLIGATIONS

What Is the Honour of the Crown?

The honour of the Crown is a constitutional principle that governments must always deal fairly and honourably with Indigenous people.

The Seven Years' War between Britain and France culminated in the Battle of Quebec on the Plains of Abraham in 1759 and the signing of the Treaty of Paris in 1763. Shortly afterward, King George III issued the Royal Proclamation of 1763. Through this unilateral declaration, Britain claimed an interest in the lands of Indigenous Peoples in what is now Canada. The courts have described this as the Crown's **de facto control** of Indigenous Peoples' land and resources, i.e. actual control of the land, in contrast to de jure control, which means control based on law or a legal right.

Through the Royal Proclamation of 1763 the British Crown ignored Indigenous sovereignty and land rights and asserted its own sovereignty without conquering Indigenous people or entering into treaties. This was the Doctrine of Discovery in action. Because it did this, there arose what the Supreme Court has described as a "tension" between Crown sovereignty and Indigenous sovereignty and rights. This tension gave rise to a "special relationship" which requires Crown representatives to always act fairly in their dealings with Indigenous people—this is what the courts refer to when they speak of the **honour of the Crown**.

According to the Supreme Court, King George III in 1763 pledged to act fairly towards Indigenous Nations not because of any sense of paternalism, but because he knew the Indigenous Nations the British were dealing with at the time were militarily strong and he wanted to convince them their interests would be better protected by relying on Britain's promises rather than going to war to protect their own interests.

The principle of the honour of the Crown is the basis for different government obligations to Indigenous people: fiduciary duty; duty to consult; justifying the infringement of **recognized rights**; duty to negotiate just settlements; duty to diligently fulfill constitutional promises; and the liberal interpretation of treaties and laws affecting Indigenous people.

The principle of the honour of the Crown embodies the awkward tension at the core of Canada's reconciliation project. It requires government to act fairly and honourably in all dealings with Indigenous people because the Crown's initial claim of control and ownership of Indigenous lands was based on unfair, dishonourable conduct with no basis in law.

Why Does the Crown Have a Duty to Consult?

The Crown has a duty to consult because it denies Indigenous rights.

Through the *Sparrow* decision (1990) and the *Badger* decision (1996), the Supreme Court put the onus on the Crown to justify the infringement of recognized Aboriginal and treaty rights. As part of justification, the Crown has to demonstrate it consulted with Indigenous people.

These decisions didn't address section 35 rights that governments deny exist. Governments and industry argued for business as usual until either treaties were agreed to or Indigenous people successfully proved their rights in a Canadian court. They argued that if Indigenous people had legitimate concerns that irreversible harm was being done to their lands while they waited, they could go to court to get an injunction to put a stop to it. But by the late 1990s, it was increasingly difficult for governments (and the courts) to justify the ongoing unilateral exploitation of Indigenous lands based simply on a denial of rights.

The Supreme Court finally addressed the issue in 2004 (see "Why Is the *Haida* Decision Important?"). It decided the law of injunctions was inadequate to protect unrecognized rights and that it would not uphold the honour of the Crown to allow federal and provincial governments to run roughshod over unrecognized Aboriginal rights while claims were making their way through the courts or treaties were being negotiated. Therefore, building on consultation obligations it had outlined in *Sparrow* and *Badger*, the Court concluded the Crown had a constitutional duty to consult and, in certain situations, accommodate Indigenous people before their rights were recognized by governments or the courts. In essence, the Court developed duty to consult law to throw a cloak of legitimacy over colonization.

What Is Required to Fulfill the Duty to Consult?

Requirements to fulfill the duty to consult depend on how strong a claim the Indigenous people have to a section 35 right, the importance of a recognized Aboriginal or treaty right, and how serious the potential effect is of the contemplated Crown conduct.

It is important to not confuse the duty to consult and accommodate with the government's responsibility to consult the general public. Unlike general consultation responsibilities, the duty to consult is a constitutional obligation. The Supreme Court has described it as a constitutional imperative (see "Why Is the *Clyde River* Decision Important?"). It is a mandatory obligation based on the highest Canadian law. Consultation responsibilities exist on a spectrum, from minimal responsibilities to the most demanding. The stronger the claim and the more serious the potential effect on the Aboriginal right, the more onerous the Crown's responsibilities in fulfilling the duty to consult (see "Why Is the *Haida* Decision Important?").

At a minimum, consultation must begin at an early stage. It requires notice and sharing of information. Government officials must have the good faith intention and ability to address Indigenous concerns. There must be a willingness to abandon the project if necessary. If the project proceeds, government officials must revise plans based on Indigenous proposals or explain why they've been rejected. While there is no duty to agree, consultation must be more than an opportunity for Indigenous people to blow off steam. Indigenous people cannot take unreasonable positions that frustrate good faith efforts to consult with them, but they can engage in hard bargaining.

When there is a strong claim and serious potential effects on title and rights, government may be required to do much more than meet minimum requirements. Governments may be required to change proposals, work with Indigenous people to find stopgap solutions to minimize adverse effects and involve them in decision-making. In the most serious cases, the consent of Indigenous people may be required. As more information is shared during consultation, the government may need to revise upward the scope of consultation owed to Indigenous people.

Why Don't Indigenous People Have a Veto?

As long as federal and provincial governments deny Aboriginal rights and treaty rights, including Aboriginal title, in Canadian law Indigenous people do not have the authority to stop the exploitation of their lands. This is an example of the Doctrine of Discovery in operation.

Based on the assertion of Crown sovereignty, Canadian governments assume they have ultimate decision-making authority over Indigenous lands. Canadian courts support governments' monopolization of decision-making by insisting that while governments deny the existence of Aboriginal rights, Indigenous people do not have a veto, i.e. they do not have the authority to stop the exploitation of their lands (see "Why Is the *Haida* Decision Important?").

The **no-veto principle** rewards federal and provincial governments for denying the existence of Indigenous rights. As long as they maintain their denial, they can proceed as if they have ultimate decision-making authority. This allows them to force through projects that exploit Indigenous lands as long as they meet the procedural requirements for consultation.

Even when they don't meet their consultation obligations, they can assume few First Nations will have the resources to pursue a legal challenge. For those who do, if the government has checked all the required consultation boxes, succeeding in court is a daunting challenge for a First Nation. This is because governments and industry consistently play the "no-veto" card and because the courts give government decision-makers a wide degree of latitude when making a decision.

If the First Nation manages to overcome all these obstacles and convince a judge the government failed to properly consult, judges often grant governments a mulligan and allow them a do-over, this time with specific direction on what further consultation they need to do to secure court approval.

Government denial and the no-veto principle work hand-in-hand to criminalize Indigenous land defenders. When Indigenous people attempt to exercise their inherent, unextinguished decision-making authority over their lands in opposition to a federal or provincial government authorization, Canadian courts grant resource-extraction companies injunctions against them. The RCMP or provincial police enforce the injunctions, often violently, and land defenders are given fines and jail sentences.

What Role Do Environmental Assessments Play in Fulfilling the Duty to Consult?

Environmental assessments are useful for information gathering but are not sufficient on their own to meet the Crown's duty to consult and accommodate obligations.

When it comes to the duty to consult, the only absolute requirement is that the Crown offer Indigenous people a process for their concerns to be considered. But the duty to consult doesn't provide Indigenous people the right to a specific, concrete outcome.

This is what the courts mean when they describe the duty to consult as a **procedural right**, i.e. it is a right to a process. It is not a substantive right such as a treaty right to hunt, a right that entitles Indigenous People to something definite—the right to harvest animals.

Since the Supreme Court's 2004 *Taku* decision, federal and provincial environmental assessments have become the standard processes for fulfilling the duty to consult. Ironically, the environmental assessment process the Court considered and approved in *Taku* had already been gutted by the BC provincial government.

The problem with environmental assessments is that they assess environmental effects. They are ill-suited to assess effects on Aboriginal and treaty rights. While there is often a connection between environmental issues and Aboriginal and treaty rights (e.g. harvesting rights), there are also section 35 rights with little direct relation to the environment (e.g. decision-making rights). Government officials tend to prioritize environmental issues and fail to appreciate the significance of their separate responsibilities to assess effects on section 35 rights (see "Why Is the *Clyde River* Decision Important?").

The Crown's ultimate responsibility is to assess potential impacts on recognized Aboriginal and treaty rights, and those the Crown continues to deny. While an environmental assessment might assist, especially for information gathering, it will rarely have all the tools and focus to fulfill the Crown's constitutional obligations. This is why the Crown must be willing to have a separate, parallel process directly with Indigenous people.

Does the Duty to Consult Include Cumulative Effects?

A new potential impact on Aboriginal and treaty rights is required to trigger the duty to consult, but once triggered the duty may include cumulative effects.

Colonization has a past, present and future. Although early court decisions on the duty to consult dealt with anticipated, planned projects, this does not mean the duty to consult is only about future impacts on Aboriginal rights.

The Supreme Court has been clear that the duty to consult is not the legal mechanism for addressing past wrongs, including previous failures to fulfill the duty to consult. As long as the status quo is maintained, i.e. there's no change to an existing, past infringement of Aboriginal or treaty rights, such as an electric transmission line built fifty years ago, there's no duty to consult.

But that's not the end of the matter. For the duty to consult to exist, the Crown must propose doing something new. There needs to be a trigger. A **trigger for the duty to consult** is any Crown action with the potential to affect Aboriginal and treaty rights. This includes obvious effects you can see, e.g. greenlighting a pipeline, as well as effects that are not visible, e.g. extending the operating permit for an existing pipeline.

When the duty to consult is triggered, whether based on new on-the-ground physical impacts on Aboriginal and treaty rights, or high-level, strategic operational changes, consultation is not necessarily limited to potential effects of the new proposed action. The existing state of affairs can't be simply ignored. The scope of consultation may need to include the cumulative effects and historical context of an existing and new project ("Why Is the *Chippewas of the Thames* Decision Important?").

An example of how this works in practice would be an electric transmission line constructed fifty years ago. As long as nothing changes, there's no duty to consult. But if there's a proposal to, say, twin the transmission line or to transfer ownership and operation to a new company, this will trigger the duty to consult. Once the duty is triggered, the existing and ongoing effects of the existing transmission line can't be ignored. Nor would it be reasonable to only consult about the effects of the proposed new transmission line. While the duty to consult is forward-looking, once triggered it does not turn a blind eye to the past.

What Is the Role of Companies in Fulfilling the Duty to Consult?

Governments might make companies responsible for assisting with fulfilling the duty to consult, but the ultimate responsibility is with the Crown.

Although the duty to consult is a Crown obligation, Indigenous people often end up engaging more with company representatives than government officials. Early on in the development of duty to consult law, there was an argument that companies owe Indigenous people a separate, legally enforceable obligation to consult. The Supreme Court rejected this argument. It decided the duty to consult is owed solely by the Crown.

But this doesn't mean there's no role for companies. The Court decided governments can delegate what it called the **procedural aspects of consultation** to companies. Presumably, this would result in companies being responsible for sharing information about a proposed project with Indigenous people, answering questions and discussing possible mitigation measures.

The challenge for First Nations, and companies, is that there's not a clear line between the procedural aspects of consultation and the real substance of the duty to consult and accommodate, which is still the responsibility of the Crown. Too often, government officials cross the line. They delegate consultation to companies holus-bolus and falsely assume their job is to simply review the company's record of consultation with First Nations and decide whether the company's consultation was adequate.

As a result, Indigenous people are often left talking to company representatives about issues far outside their scope of responsibility.

For example, as part of possible accommodation measures, many First Nations want a discussion about permitting, cumulative effects and the sharing of Crown revenues—company representatives obviously can't enter into these discussions.

Is This Consultation or Engagement?

Instead of being concerned about whether a meeting is consultation or engagement, it is preferable to focus on whether it's meaningful.

Clients often ask whether discussions with the government or companies should be considered *consultation* or *engagement*. The problem with this distinction is that it plays into the misconception that if government or company representatives meet with First Nations enough times, send enough emails and buy them enough donuts and coffees, eventually it will add up to the magic number and the Crown's consultation obligations will have been fulfilled.

Consultation isn't arithmetic. For it to be more than cynically offering Indigenous people a forum to blow off steam, it must adhere to a handful of fundamental principles. First, it must proceed from the correct basis. Government officials must understand which issues need to be on the table. If they refuse to discuss relevant issues, the entire process is bankrupt from the start. For example, if a First Nation has a credible claim to Aboriginal title, the Crown must be willing to discuss revenue sharing and decision-making. Refusing to have this discussion is likely the basis for cancelling any subsequent decision.

Second, consultation must be about more than listening to and recording Indigenous concerns. It's the duty to consult, not the duty to create a consultation log. Government officials must act in good faith. They must be honest and fair when consulting Indigenous people. They must be willing to reject a company's application. They must *actively* listen (a trait all too rare in the law) with the sincere intention of working with First Nations to find solutions to issues. If they can't address an issue themselves, they must connect the First Nation with government officials who can. If a First Nation's preferred course of action can't be supported, they must explain why not.

Performative consultation sows the seeds of cynicism. For the duty to consult to result in anything meaningful, it needs to do hard, uncomfortable work.

Why Is the Duty to Consult Inadequate?

The duty to consult is inadequate because it is based on denial.

Clients and students are often surprised I'm not a fan of the duty to consult. While it is definitely better than what preceded it (uphill attempts to convince a court to grant an injunction) and has undoubtedly established the parameters for many negotiated agreements, ultimately it is premised on the denial of Indigenous rights.

For the so-called historical treaties, First Nations are left with the duty to consult because the Crown denies they retained decision-making authority over their lands when they entered treaty. Instead, the Crown takes the position that treaty First Nations surrendered the right to decide how their lands are used. For First Nations without treaties, the duty to consult is based on the denial of all their rights and the assumption that all decision-making lies with the Crown.

Resting on a foundation of denial, the duty to consult entitles Indigenous people to no more than a process. As the courts have endlessly repeated, First Nations don't have a veto and the Crown is not obligated to agree to anything. Unless the consultation process is wholly misguided, First Nations are obligated to participate. If they don't, companies and the Crown argue in court that their unwillingness to engage "frustrated" consultation.

The handful of First Nations able to cobble together enough resources to challenge a Crown decision in court face a difficult battle. Governments and companies convince judges to only review the record created as part of the consultation process—context and the Indigenous perspective are rarely considered. The consultation process needs to be no more than adequate. The government decision-maker is granted a wide degree of deference. Their decision only needs to fall somewhere on the spectrum of a reasonable outcome, i.e. it will pass muster as long as it's not obviously groundless.

If reconciliation is going to be about substance instead of process, it needs to extend beyond the duty to consult. It needs to begin with recognition, including recognizing First Nations', both treaty and non-treaty, decision-making authority.

When Does the Crown Owe Indigenous People a Fiduciary Duty?

A fiduciary duty exists when the Crown has the power to decide how a First Nation's legal interests are managed or disposed of.

The Crown's **fiduciary duty** is based on the principle of the honour of the Crown. A fiduciary duty is potentially a powerful tool for holding government to account because it can be enforced by Canadian courts (see "Why Is the *Guerin* Decision Important?"). Most of the law of fiduciary duty has developed based on obligations owed to First Nations.

Courts refer to the wider "fiduciary relationship" between the Crown and Indigenous people, but a fiduciary duty only exists under specific, limited circumstances. The most common way for the Crown to owe a fiduciary duty is when it assumes control of a First Nation's legal interest in something, e.g. reserve lands, and has the power to decide how it's managed, e.g. leasing reserve lands. The legal term is discretionary control of a **cognizable interest**.

Not every interaction between the Crown and Indigenous people results in the Crown owing Indigenous people a fiduciary duty (see "Why Is the *Wewaykum* Decision Important?"). Arguments by Indigenous people that a fiduciary duty exists often fail on one of two grounds. The courts decide there was no cognizable interest at stake, i.e. it wasn't an interest a Canadian court recognizes and can make a decision about. This is an example of how when seeking justice, Indigenous people are subject to the Canadian legal system. Circumstances that might give rise to legal obligations under Indigenous Peoples' own laws may not be recognized under Canadian law.

If Indigenous people surmount this first obstacle and establish that a cognizable interest exists, the courts might decide there is insufficient evidence the Crown had **discretionary control** of the interest, i.e. it didn't have ultimate decision-making over the interest. Most successful fiduciary duty cases are based on the Crown's mismanagement of reserve lands or money held in trust for a First Nation.

What Are the Crown's Obligations When It Owes a Fiduciary Duty?

When a fiduciary duty exists, the Crown's specific obligations will be different depending on the Indigenous legal interest at stake.

The general rule is that a fiduciary must manage and protect a beneficiary's property as an ordinary person would if the property belonged to them, i.e. they must act in the beneficiary's best interests. But when the Crown is a fiduciary for Indigenous people, it can get much more complicated.

When a fiduciary duty exists, it does not mean the Crown is obligated to compensate Indigenous people for any and all losses. Instead, the Crown owes specific obligations based on the type of Indigenous legal interest at stake and the importance of that legal interest to the Indigenous people.

For example, the Supreme Court decided the Crown's obligations to a First Nation were less burdensome when an Indian Act reserve was proposed to be created but had not yet been confirmed. After the reserve had been officially established, the Crown's fiduciary duty was more onerous (see "Why Is the *Wewaykum* Decision Important?"). If the Crown intends to expropriate reserve lands, the fiduciary duty includes a requirement that it take no more than necessary to achieve its purpose (see "Why Is the *Osoyoos* Decision Important?").

In most cases when a person owes a fiduciary duty, e.g. a trustee who makes decisions about a child's property, the fiduciary's sole responsibility is to the person whose property they control. The Crown often finds itself in a more complicated situation because it might owe a First Nation a fiduciary duty, but also have responsibilities to the wider public or to another First Nation.

For example, when Indian Act reserves were being created, but had not yet been finally established, the Crown could owe obligations to one or more First Nations and to non-Indigenous people who were coveting "Crown land." In that situation, the Crown couldn't just play the role of an honest referee. Instead, the Crown's fiduciary duty included loyalty, acting in good faith, fully disclosing all information and using ordinary care to protect the First Nation's interests.

But when the legal interest is different, so is the fiduciary duty. For example, when the Crown has the ultimate power over the proposed surrender of an established Indian Act reserve, it must ensure the Indian Act band is allowed to decide on the surrender and to ensure the terms of the surrender are fair and reasonable.

How Does the Crown Avoid Responsibility for Breaching a Fiduciary Duty?

When the Crown breaches a fiduciary duty to Indigenous people, there are several legal arguments it relies on to avoid responsibility for its wrongs.

Even when the Crown breaches a fiduciary duty to Indigenous people, it doesn't necessarily mean it has to do anything about it. The Crown can avoid responsibility in various ways.

The Crown might argue the Indigenous people took too long to file their claim in court and so, based on time limits created by the federal Parliament or the provincial legislatures, a court cannot force the Crown to do anything—this is called limitation periods.

Because self-serving limitation periods are patently unfair to First Nations who have suffered because of the Crown breaching its fiduciary duty, a recent development has been for the courts, in certain situations, to make declarations that the Crown has breached the honour of the Crown. These types of declarations are not enforceable, so whether they have any practical utility is open to question (see "Why Is the *Manitoba Métis* Decision Important?").

Limitation periods are not the only way the Crown can avoid the consequences of breaching a fiduciary duty to Indigenous people. The Crown can rely on the fact that under Canadian law it's ultimately up to the courts to decide whether in the particular circumstances the Crown will be held to account. For example, the Crown might convince a judge the Indigenous people knew about the wrong and took so long to complain that it had reasonably concluded they had given their okay.

If that argument fails, the Crown might convince a judge it would simply be unfair to force it to do anything after so much time had passed without the Indigenous people making any formal complaints about the Crown's misconduct. Two examples of judges accepting this type of argument include the Court in the 1980s rejecting Temagami First Nation's claim that they were not a party to the Robinson Huron Treaty of 1850, and the Court in 2000 rejecting the claim from Aamjiwnaang First Nation (formerly known as the Chippewas of Sarnia) that there had been an illegal surrender of their reserve in 1840.

Are Indigenous Rights Trumped by the Public Interest?

The public interest cannot trump Indigenous peoples' constitutionally protected rights.

When governments make decisions, they are often responsible for ensuring the decision is in the public interest; for example, building a pipeline or giving the greenlight to a new mine. Ever since the Supreme Court began interpreting the purpose and scope of section 35, it has been faced with arguments that would limit Aboriginal rights based on the greater importance of the so-called public interest.

Beginning with the earliest section 35 decisions, the Court has scolded governments for simple-mindedly pleading "the public interest" as a defence for overriding section 35 rights. The Court said the public interest was simply too vague, broad and unworkable to be an excuse for trampling on Aboriginal rights (see "Why Is the *Sparrow* Decision Important?" and "Why Is the *Van der Peet* Decision Important?").

The Court has also rejected arguments that the public interest trumps its fiduciary responsibilities to Indigenous people. The Crown can wear "many hats." It can act as a fiduciary and also protect the public interest—these roles aren't incompatible. One way it can do this is to first decide if a project or authorization is in the public interest and then consider what, in the circumstances, is required to uphold its fiduciary responsibilities to Indigenous people (see "Why Is the *Guerin* Decision Important?", "Why Is the *Osoyoos* Decision Important?" and "Why Is the *Southwind* Decision Important?").

Federal and provincial administrative tribunals (e.g. the Ontario Energy Board) must also ensure their decisions are in the public interest. The Supreme Court has repeatedly confirmed that in these situations, duty to consult can't be trumped by the public interest. The Court has explained that a contract or approval that breaches constitutional duties or constitutionally protected rights simply cannot be in the public interest (see "Why Is the *Rio Tinto* Decision Important?" and "Why Is the *Clyde River* Decision Important?").

Another way to think of this question is to imagine the Crown's constitutional obligations to Indigenous people as being upstream from any decision made under a federal or provincial law. A government official responsible for fulfilling the duty to consult must first decide whether constitutional obligations have been fulfilled. If they have, they proceed in their role as government decision-maker making a decision under the specific terms of the federal or provincial law. If, on the other hand, they decide the constitutional obligations have not been fulfilled, they can't proceed. As the Supreme Court has said more than once, the duty to consult is a constitutional imperative—it can't be left unfulfilled.

RECONCILIATION

What Is Reconciliation?

Reconciliation is Canada's attempt to legitimize its ongoing colonization project.

The Truth and Reconciliation Commission described reconciliation as a process establishing and maintaining respectful relationships between Indigenous and non-Indigenous peoples.

In contrast, the Supreme Court's definition of reconciliation has focussed on the need, and the process, for resolving the tension between Indigenous Peoples' pre-existing rights to their lands and waters, with the assumed sovereignty and property rights of the colonizers and their descendants.

The legal process of reconciliation includes the need for governments to justify the infringement of Aboriginal and treaty rights. It also includes the requirement to consult, and if necessary, accommodate Indigenous people when a course of action or decision affects Aboriginal and treaty rights.

In recent years the Supreme Court has increasingly described reconciliation as a process for balancing Indigenous and non-Indigenous interests while acknowledging that non-Indigenous interests might not have a basis in law.

What Is the "Indian Problem"?

There is no "Indian Problem"—the problem is Canada.

Non-Indigenous people often focus on what they see as problems Indigenous people face, e.g. poverty, governance, violence, alcoholism, etc. They fail to understand that what they are describing are the effects of Canada's ongoing racist and violent colonization project.

The long history of non-Indigenous people offering solutions to the "Indian problem" is deeply embedded in Canadian history and government policy. It is based on the racist assumption that European political, legal and cultural practices are the ideal and Indigenous societies are inherently inferior.

This assumption came to the fore in the early and mid-nineteenth century as part of government attempts to assimilate Indigenous people. It led directly to Canada's genocidal residential school regime. It continues to inform government policy and legislation, e.g. the federal First Nation Financial Transparency Act.

There are many historical and contemporary examples of the concept of the "Indian problem" being weaponized to displace and oppress Indigenous people. For example, Canadian law and politicians often point to Indigenous people's supposed underuse of their lands to justify removing them and overriding their laws and values in favour of exploitation of the land for the benefit of non-Indigenous people.

To forge a new way forward, instead of asking how to solve the "Indian problem," Canadians need to focus on how to solve the problems with Canadian law and policy that justify and support the displacement and marginalization of Indigenous people.

Why Is the Royal Commission on Aboriginal Peoples Important?

The Royal Commission on Aboriginal Peoples is important because it detailed the effects of Canada's genocidal policies towards Indigenous people and laid a framework for a new, respectful relationship.

In the 1990s the so-called Oka Crisis was the most prominent, but not the only example of Indigenous people continuing their ancestors' tradition of taking direct action to defend their land and rights. In response, the federal government created the Royal Commission on Aboriginal Peoples in 1991 to study Indigenous people's frustration with Canada's ongoing colonization project and make recommendations for changing Canada's laws and policies.

The commission's 1996 multi-volume report called for a thorough revamping of Canada's relationship with Indigenous people. In place of the country's failed assimilation and removal policies, the commission called for the reconstitution of Indigenous Nations with their own law-making powers and functioning economies based on control of their land and resources.

The commission's influence on the thinking of Supreme Court judges has been uneven. The Court has frequently relied on the commission's report to highlight the destructive effects of Canada's residential school system, systemic racism in the criminal justice system, and the importance of treaties. The Court recently relied on the commission's report as support for the federal government's use of legislation to recognize Indigenous self-government rights (see "Why Is the *C-92 Reference* Decision Important?").

The Supreme Court's selective reliance on the commission's report has seen it cite the commission to justify limitations on Indigenous self-government rights (see "Why Is the *Mitchell* Decision Important?") while ignoring aspects of the commission's report that question the legitimacy of the Canadian state, including the Doctrine of Discovery (see "Why Is the *Tsilhqot'in* Decision Important?"). The Court's most glaring inconsistency has been its willingness to lean on the commission's report to describe treaties as the basis of solemn promises (see "Why Is the *Shot Both Sides* Decision Important?") but at the same time ignoring the commission's description of treaties as agreements to share the land. Despite the commission's clear direction, the Court continues to describe treaties as agreements to surrender the land (see "Why Is the *Grassy Narrows* Decision Important?" and "Why Is the Supreme Court's *Restoule* Decision Important?").

Why Is the Truth and Reconciliation Commission Important?

The Truth and Reconciliation Commission is important because its work exposed the racism and violence at the heart of Canada's ongoing colonization.

The Royal Commission on Aboriginal Peoples called for a public inquiry into Canada's residential school system. The Truth and Reconciliation Commission was created as part of the settlement of class-action lawsuits brought on behalf of survivors of Canada's residential school system. The commission spent six years collecting evidence of the residential school system and hearing from survivors and family members, as well as church and government employees. The summary of its multi-volume final report, *Honouring the Truth, Reconciling for the Future*, released in 2015, is over five hundred pages and includes ninety-four "Calls to Action" aimed at redressing the legacy of residential schools and advancing reconciliation. Its records are maintained by the National Centre for Truth and Reconciliation.

The commission's findings on the extent of the abuse and violence experienced by Indigenous children in the so-called school system, which it described as "cultural genocide," came as a shock to many non-Indigenous Canadians. It upset their accepted view of Canada as the "good colonizer" in comparison to other countries, including the United States. While most Canadians have accepted the truth of the commission's report, many continue to underplay or deny the commission's findings and wide-scale suffering of Indigenous children.

As explained by the commission, the residential school system was rooted in Canadian society's racist and paternalistic policies toward Indigenous people. The racism and paternalism that justified the violence perpetuated against Indigenous children, their families and communities was not limited to residential schools. It has also been a central factor in the development of Aboriginal law. The continued centrality of the Doctrine of Discovery in Canadian law, based on the racist assumption of the superiority of "civilized" Europeans in comparison to Indigenous "savages," is an obvious example.

Reconciliation requires exposing, disrupting and uprooting these attitudes throughout the systems, policies and laws that dominate, marginalize and disentitle current and future generations of Indigenous people.

Why Is the United Nations Declaration on the Rights of Indigenous Peoples Important?

The United Nations Declaration on the Rights of Indigenous Peoples is important because it is another tool for holding governments to account when they do not fulfill their commitments to Indigenous people.

After nearly twenty-five years of debate, the United Nations Declaration on the Rights of Indigenous Peoples was adopted by the United Nations in 2007 as a set of minimum standards for the survival of Indigenous Peoples. The declaration's forty-six articles include a wide range of commitments by member states to protect Indigenous culture, languages, customs, religions and right to self-determination. One hundred and forty-four countries voted to adopt the declaration. Four countries voted against it, including Australia, Canada, New Zealand and the United States.

Canada's opposition was based on its concern that adopting the declaration would threaten federal and provincial governments' exclusive authority to make decisions on the use and exploitation of Indigenous lands and resources. The federal government and corporate supporters mounted a disinformation campaign alleging the declaration's commitment to Indigenous Peoples' right to free, prior and informed consent was equivalent to a veto that would undermine Canada's economy.

After further consideration, Canadian governments realized they could pass aspirational legislation committing to implement the declaration without running the risk of giving up control over Indigenous lands. In 2019 British Columbia was the first to step forward with legislation. Canada passed similar legislation in 2021. Despite all the political rhetoric that accompanied their enactment, to date Canadian courts have expressed doubt that the British Columbia and federal legislation promising to implement the declaration created any new legally enforceable obligations.

As important as the declaration might be in the long term for directing the national conversation towards issues too little discussed (see *Article 28* and the right to redress for the confiscation of Indigenous lands), on its own it can't be expected to solve the underlying flaws in Canada's reconciliation project. It's not a shortage of legal obligations that frustrates reconciliation—it is federal and provincial governments' refusal to fulfill existing legal obligations and the courts' growing reluctance to enforce them.

What Is "Land Back"?

Land Back is about recognizing Indigenous Peoples' inherent authority over their lands.

The **Land Back** movement requires Canadians to recognize the fundamental lie at the basis of the Canadian state—the lie that colonizers have simply claimed Indigenous land as their own and relegated Indigenous people to making a claim for their own land. Land Back is also about forging new relationships between Indigenous Nations and the Crown that create space for Indigenous people to exercise their inherent rights and responsibilities to make decisions about their lands and benefit from them.

It is important to understand what Land Back isn't. Land Back isn't about using established legal mechanisms based on the assumption of Crown sovereignty. For example, adding land to Indian Act reserves isn't Land Back. Additions to reserves, while important for individual First Nations, are based on an acceptance of Canada's claim to Indigenous land. When lands are added to reserves, legally they are owned by the federal government for the use and benefit of an Indian Act band of "Indians." This isn't Land Back.

Land Back also isn't about transferring land through modern-day treaties. The entire premise of Canada's comprehensive claims process is contrary to Land Back because it is based on the assumption that colonizers have a legitimate claim to Indigenous land and Indigenous Nations must accept limited rights over a small percentage of their territory in exchange for surrendering their rights to the majority of their territory.

Aboriginal title also isn't about Land Back. Aboriginal title is an interest in land created by Canadian courts that denies Indigenous People's inherent rights and responsibilities. It is based on essentializing Indigenous people, has significant limits and can be infringed, i.e. extinguished, by the Crown, for a multitude of purposes (see "What Is Aboriginal title?").

Land Back is about rejecting the lie of the Doctrine of Discovery. It is about accepting that Indigenous Nations have law-making authority over their lands. Land Back is about negotiating Crown-Indigenous agreements that establish a relationship that recognizes and puts into effect this reality.

SECTION II

The Top 50 Aboriginal Law Decisions and Why They Are Important

ABORIGINAL TITLE

Why Is the *St. Catherine's Milling* Decision Important?

Aboriginal Title – Doctrine of Discovery

The Privy Council's St. Catherine's Milling *decision in 1888 is important because it was the first major Canadian court case to consider the relationship between Indigenous Peoples' legal interests in their lands and the legal interests of the federal and provincial governments.*

St. Catherine's Milling was the result of a dispute between the federal and Ontario governments over logging rights in northwestern Ontario—Indigenous Peoples were not directly involved. The federal government argued the lands had been owned by the Anishinaabe and that their land rights had passed to the federal government through Treaty 3. Ontario insisted that it held title to the lands.

The case was ultimately heard by the Judicial Committee of the Privy Council in London, which was the highest court for Canadian legal disputes until 1949.

The Privy Council relied on the Doctrine of Discovery from earlier US Supreme Court decisions to conclude that the Crown had acquired the underlying title to all Indigenous lands in Canada. As between Ontario and the federal government, the Province now owned all Indigenous Peoples' lands, except Indian reserves.

The Canadian Supreme Court has continued to rely on the doctrine and *St. Catherine's Milling* as fundamental to its interpretation of section 35 of the constitution (see "Why Is the *Sparrow* Decision Important?" and "Why Is the *Van der Peet* Decision Important?").

Why Is the *Calder* Decision Important?

Aboriginal Title – Aboriginal Rights – Basis For

The Supreme Court's 1973 Calder decision is important because it confirmed Aboriginal rights are derived from Indigenous Peoples' occupation of their lands before colonizers arrived.

In the late 1960s, the Nisga'a asked the court to declare that their Aboriginal title to over one thousand square miles of their territory in northwestern British Columbia continued to exist, despite over one hundred years of colonization.

Three members of the Supreme Court decided Nisga'a Aboriginal title no longer existed because it was incompatible with the Crown's obvious intent to exercise complete control over Nisga'a land.

Three judges concluded that since there was no evidence of the Crown's intention to do away with Nisga'a title, it might still exist.

The seventh judge, supported by the first three, concluded the Nisga'a's claim should be dismissed because the Nisga'a had not received permission from the Province of British Columbia to file their lawsuit.

Nonetheless, *Calder* established that Aboriginal title, if it did exist, was based on Indigenous Peoples' pre-existing right to the land and not on the Crown's favour or generosity.

The most quoted words from the decision were written by one of the judges who rejected the Nisga'a's claim: "the fact is that when the settlers came, the Indians were there, organized in societies and occupying the land as their forefathers had done for centuries."

In response to the decision, Prime Minister Pierre Trudeau reportedly told a group of chiefs, "Maybe you have more rights than we thought." In the wake of *Calder*, the federal government changed its policy regarding Aboriginal title and rights to allow for the negotiation of "land claims" with Indigenous Peoples.

Why Is the *Delgamuukw* Decision Important?

Aboriginal Title – Proof & Content

The Supreme Court's 1997 Delgamuukw *decision is important because it clarified what Aboriginal title is and what is required to prove it in court.*

At trial, the Gitxsan and the Wet'suwet'en sought recognition of their respective nations' ownership and jurisdiction over approximately 58,000 square kilometres in northwestern British Columbia. The Supreme Court considered their arguments as a claim for Aboriginal title.

In *Delgamuukw* (also known as *Delgamuukw-Gisday'wa*) the Court decided the rules of evidence had to be adapted to allow for the consideration of Indigenous Peoples' oral histories. The Court also decided Aboriginal title is not simply a bundle of harvesting rights: it is a right to the land itself. It includes the right to benefit from the land and the right to decide how the land is used or not used.

Implicitly relying on the Doctrine of Discovery, the Court assumed Crown title to Indigenous lands was established through the **assertion of Crown sovereignty**. Consequently, to prove Aboriginal title, an Indigenous Nation must prove its exclusive occupation of the land before the assertion of Crown sovereignty. Occupation might be proven through physical occupation or the existence of Indigenous laws over the land.

The Court held that while Aboriginal title could not have been extinguished by provincial laws prior to the Constitution Act in 1982, the Crown might be able to infringe it for a wide range of reasons including mining, hydroelectricity, the settlement of foreign populations, etc.

Because the nations had argued at trial for ownership and jurisdiction instead of Aboriginal title, the Court decided a new trial was necessary. The new trial has never been held. In 2014 the Tsilhqot'in, building on the *Delgamuukw* decision, succeeded in obtaining the first declaration of Aboriginal title in Canadian history (see "Why Is the *Tsilhqot'in* Decision Important?").

Why Is the *Tsilhqot'in* Decision Important?

Aboriginal Title – Infringement

The Supreme Court's 2014 Tsilhqot'in decision is important because it resulted in the first Aboriginal title declaration in Canadian history.

In the late 1980s, the Xeni Gwet'in, part of the Tsilhqot'in Nation, sought to stop commercial logging in the Nemiah Valley in northern British Columbia. Following the 1997 *Delgamuukw* decision, they amended their legal action to include a claim for Aboriginal title.

In *Tsilhqot'in*, the Supreme Court applied the test for Aboriginal title from *Delgamuukw* and resolved confusion it had sowed in an earlier 2005 decision, *Marshall & Bernard*: Aboriginal title is not restricted to specific sites, e.g. salt licks and buffalo jumps; it can apply to wider territorial claims.

Also, the Court abandoned the rule that "local settler majorities," i.e. provinces, cannot apply their laws to issues of fundamental importance to Indigenous Peoples, i.e. rights and land. This principle, dating back to the Royal Proclamation of 1763, had been confirmed by the Court as recently as 2006 in the *Morris* decision. Instead, the Court held that provinces can, if justified, infringe Aboriginal title.

The Court's confirmation that the Tsilhqot'in hold Aboriginal title over a portion of their territory was an important victory for the Tsilhqot'in and all Indigenous Peoples. Since the decision, other Indigenous Peoples have filed title claims raising issues left unresolved in *Tsilhqot'in*, e.g. title to private lands and lands under water. These claims have not yet reached the Supreme Court.

Since the decision, the Tsilhqot'in have been in negotiations with BC and Canada to implement their title. Other Indigenous Peoples have sought to engage with Canada and provinces to reach agreement on implementing their title without the cost, risk and delay of going through the courts (e.g. the 2024 Haida Nation Title Land Agreement and legislation).

ABORIGINAL RIGHTS

Why Is the *Sparrow* Decision Important?

Aboriginal Rights – Purpose of Section 35

The 1990 Sparrow *decision is important because it was the Supreme Court's first confirmation of an Aboriginal right under section 35 of the constitution.*

In 1984, two years after constitutional protection for existing Aboriginal and treaty rights had been enshrined in section 35 of the constitution, Musqueam member Ron Sparrow was charged for fishing in the Fraser River with a net longer than allowed under federal law. In court, Sparrow argued the law interfered with Musqueam's constitutionally protected Aboriginal right to fish.

The Supreme Court decided section 35 was intended to provide Indigenous Peoples with limited protection from government regulation for certain activities, e.g. fishing. The protection is not absolute. Even a protected Aboriginal right can be limited or regulated.

The Court also decided the constitution only protects Aboriginal rights in existence when section 35 came into effect in 1982. If a right had been extinguished before 1982, it was not renewed and protected.

Government regulation of an Aboriginal right before 1982 did not mean the right had been extinguished. Extinguishment could only have occurred if there was evidence of the Crown's clear and plain intent to do so.

The Court rejected the argument that Musqueam's Aboriginal fishing right was equivalent to property rights of non-Indigenous people. Also, the Court accepted without question the underlying premise of the Doctrine of Discovery. It acknowledged the law had long recognized Indigenous Peoples might have a right to occupy parts of their territory, but claimed "there was from the outset never any doubt that sovereignty and legislative power, and indeed the underlying title, to such lands vested in the Crown."

The Court decided Musqueam had proven its right to a food, social and ceremonial fishery and that subject to conservation, this Musqueam fishery had priority over other fisheries.

In response to the *Sparrow* decision, the federal government introduced the Aboriginal Fisheries Strategy to regulate First Nations' food, social and ceremonial fisheries.

Why Is the *Nikal* Decision Important?

Aboriginal Rights – Indian Reserves

The Supreme Court's 1996 Nikal decision is important because it restricted British Columbia First Nations' access to their traditional fisheries in rivers running through their reserves.

In the summer of 1986, Jerry Nikal, a member of Witset (formerly Moricetown) First Nation, fished for salmon from the banks of the Bulkley River in northwestern BC. Despite fishing from reserve lands in a river that ran through his First Nation's reserve, Nikal was charged under federal legislation for fishing without a licence. Nikal argued that because he was fishing within his reserve, he only had to comply with his First Nation's fishing by-law and that the federal government's licence requirement was an infringement of his Aboriginal right to fish.

Justice Cory, for the majority of the Court, concluded that although the First Nation had an Aboriginal fishing right, the setting aside of the reserve on both sides of the Bulkley River did not mean that they had the right to an exclusive fishery. In an unusual and controversial departure from standard court practice, Justice Cory came to this conclusion based largely on his review of historical documents filed by the Canadian National Railway Company, which had intervened in the case at the Supreme Court.

He also concluded that the Bulkley River as it ran through the reserve was navigable, therefore, based on the common law, the First Nation did not have an exclusive right in the fishery.

Justice Cory also emphasized that the simple requirement for a licence will not by itself constitute an infringement of the Aboriginal right because a licensing scheme was essential for the Crown to regulate and preserve natural resources and because licences helped identify who had a right to exercise Aboriginal rights.

But, in this case, the mandatory conditions of the federal fishing licence equalled an infringement of the Aboriginal fishery right and the federal government had not presented any evidence justifying the infringement. Consequently, Nikal was acquitted of the charges.

The *Nikal* decision remains notable as an example of the Supreme Court's willingness in the mid-1990s to stretch the rules of court to justify denying Indigenous rights.

Why Is the *Van der Peet* Decision Important?

Aboriginal Rights – Legal Test

The Supreme Court's 1996 Van der Peet *decision is important because it established the legal test for recognizing Aboriginal rights under section 35 of the Constitution.*

Stó:lō Nation member Dorothy Van der Peet was charged under the federal Fisheries Act for selling ten salmon caught under a food fishery licence. Van der Peet's defence was that the federal law was invalid because it infringed her section 35 Aboriginal right to sell fish.

A majority of the Court rejected the argument that section 35 Aboriginal rights are based on Indigenous Peoples' pre-existing legal rights. Instead, it relied on the discredited United States Marshall Court decisions of the 1830s to conclude that the purpose of section 35 is to protect pre-contact practices, customs and traditions integral to an Indigenous People's distinctive culture by translating them into Aboriginal rights.

The Court held that the pre-contact exchange of fish for other goods was not a defining or central aspect of Stó:lō society. Instead, it was no more than incidental to fishing for food. Therefore, trading or selling fish did not qualify as an Aboriginal right protected under section 35 and consequently, Van der Peet was found guilty of violating the Fisheries Act.

Two Supreme Court justices wrote detailed dissenting reasons criticizing the majority of the Court for its "frozen rights" approach to Aboriginal rights and for ignoring the importance of Indigenous legal orders. Their criticisms have been echoed by many critics ever since, but the Court's focus on section 35 being intended to protect "Aboriginality" persists (see "Why Is the *Dickson* Decision Important?").

Why Is the *Gladstone* Decision Important?

Aboriginal Rights – Commercial Rights

The 1996 Gladstone decision is important because for the first time, the Supreme Court considered whether to impose a limit on commercial rights protected by section 35.

Donald and William Gladstone, members of the Heiltsuk Nation, were charged for attempting to sell herring spawn on kelp caught without a licence from the federal government. The Gladstones' defence was that the licence requirement infringed their section 35 commercial fishery right.

The Court concluded the Heiltsuk possessed a commercial fishing right protected under section 35, and sent the matter back for a new trial on the question of whether the government's allocation of herring was justifiable. An important issue for the Court was whether there was any space in the commercial fishery for non-Aboriginal fishermen or whether the commercial fishery belonged exclusively to the Heiltsuk.

The Court had earlier decided that Aboriginal rights have priority over non-Indigenous interests (*Sparrow*). Prioritization of an Indigenous food, social and ceremonial fishery did not raise the issue of an exclusive Aboriginal fishery because there was an inherent limit to the Aboriginal food fishery, i.e. there was only so much fish Indigenous people could use for food, social and ceremonial purposes.

But in *Gladstone*, the Court speculated that if an Aboriginal commercial fishing right was given priority, it could lead to an exclusive Aboriginal commercial fishery, i.e. Aboriginal fishers would catch all the fish available for sale and leave none for non-Aboriginal commercial fishers. To avoid this possibility, the Court decided that while the government had to demonstrate it had considered the existence and importance of the Aboriginal commercial fishing right, it could also allocate a commercial fishery to non-Indigenous fishers.

The Court concluded it was okay to limit Aboriginal rights that do not have an inherent limit because limiting Aboriginal rights was part and parcel of reconciliation. Also, placing limits on Aboriginal rights was justified to support the broader political, social and economic community, which included Indigenous people. The Court's "inherent limit" reasoning was later used in *Marshall* to limit the Mi'kmaq commercial fishing treaty right.

Why Is the *N.T.C. Smokehouse* Decision Important?

Aboriginal Rights – Commercial Rights

The Supreme Court's 1996 N.T.C. Smokehouse decision is important because it was an early example of the Supreme Court's reasoning for denying section 35 commercial rights.

In the fall of 1986, a British Columbia food processing company named N.T.C. Smokehouse was charged under federal legislation for purchasing and selling salmon caught by eighty members of the Tseshaht First Nation and Hupačasath First Nation under Indian food fish licences. The company argued that Tseshaht and Hupačasath had a section 35 Aboriginal right to sell the fish.

The *N.T.C. Smokehouse* appeal was argued at the Supreme Court at the same time as *Van der Peet* and *Gladstone*, and all three decisions were released at the same time.

Chief Justice Lamer, for a majority of the Supreme Court, concluded Tseshaht and Hupačasath did not have an Aboriginal right to exchange fish for money or other goods. He did so without an elaborate analysis. Instead, he relied on the trial judge's finding that before contact with Europeans, Tseshaht and Hupačasath members' sales of fish were "few and far between." Consequently, based on the *Van der Peet* test, selling fish before contact was not integral to the distinctive cultures of the Tseshaht and Hupačasath and did not qualify as an Aboriginal right.

N.T.C. Smokehouse is notable for how it contrasts with the Court's decision in *Nikal*. The two appeals were heard in the fall of 1995 during the same week by the same judges. In *N.T.C. Smokehouse*, Justice Lamer's uncritical acceptance of the trial judge's findings of fact justified denying Tseshaht's and Hupačasath's right to a commercial fishery. In *Nikal*, Justice Cory reviewed historical documents not part of the trial to deny the Witset First Nation's Aboriginal fishing right.

Despite the outcome in *N.T.C. Smokehouse*, Tseshaht's and Hupačasath's right to a commercial fishery was eventually confirmed in *Ahousaht* in 2009.

Why Is the *Pamajewon* Decision Important?

Aboriginal Rights – Self-government

The Supreme Court's 1996 Pamajewon *decision is important because it exemplifies how the law of Aboriginal rights works to defeat Indigenous self-governance.*

In the late 1980s, Eagle Lake First Nation and Shawanaga First Nation enacted on-reserve lottery laws based on their inherent rights. Members of each First Nation were later charged under the Criminal Code for illegal gambling. At the Supreme Court, the First Nations argued their lottery laws were based on their self-government rights and were protected by section 35 of the constitution.

The Court found against the First Nations. It reasoned that even if section 35 of the constitution protects self-government rights (a question the Court left unanswered), they could only be made out based on the test it had recently established in the *Van der Peet* decision.

This meant the task of the Court was to reduce the First Nations' claim to a specific activity and then determine, based on the evidence, whether at the time of contact with Europeans that activity was an integral or defining aspect of the First Nation's culture.

The Court rejected as overly general the First Nations' arguments that their right was a right to manage their reserve lands. Instead, the Court narrowed the right in question to participating in and regulating gambling on their reserve lands. Having recharacterized the right into one the First Nations had not argued at trial, unsurprisingly, the Court found there was insufficient evidence to establish the right.

Pamajewon is an example of how the Supreme Court created a test for Aboriginal rights that does not threaten the ongoing operation of the Doctrine of Discovery. Indigenous people can bring claims to the Court based on their own laws and inherent rights, but the narrowness of the *Van der Peet* test means their claims will most likely fail.

Why Are the *Adams* and *Côté* Decisions Important?

Aboriginal Rights – Infringement

The Supreme Court's 1996 Adams *and* Côté *decisions are important because they established that Aboriginal rights can exist without proving Aboriginal title to the land.*

George Adams, a Mohawk from Akwesasne, was charged for fishing without a provincial licence on Lake St. Francis, part of the St. Lawrence River in western Quebec. His defence was based on his Aboriginal right to fish protected under section 35.

In *Côté*, five members of the Kitigan Zibi Anishinabeg led a group of young people from their community northwest of Montreal to teach them traditional hunting and fishing methods. They were convicted under a provincial law for entering a controlled wilderness zone without paying a vehicle licence fee. One of them was also convicted under the federal Fisheries Act for fishing without a licence. They appealed based on Algonquin Aboriginal and treaty rights.

The two decisions were released at the same time and should be read together.

The Court decided that even if an Indigenous People may not be able to demonstrate occupation of land sufficient to prove Aboriginal title, they can still make out a claim to Aboriginal rights, e.g. hunting, fishing and trapping. But, Aboriginal rights cannot be exercised anywhere—they are limited to specific tracts of land or territories (see "What Does 'Site-specific' Mean?").

The decisions are also important for establishing what in Aboriginal law is referred to as the ***Adams* point**. This is the legal principle that if a provincial or federal law allows a decision-maker to exercise discretion as to whether to allow Indigenous people to exercise an Aboriginal right, the law must include specific criteria for exercising that discretion. If it doesn't, this is itself an infringement of the Aboriginal right. While technically *Côté* wasn't a complete victory, in essence both it and the *Adams* decisions were important wins for First Nations.

Why Is the *Mitchell* Decision Important?

Aboriginal Rights – Taxation

The Supreme Court's 2001 Mitchell decision is important because it demonstrates how courts recharacterize Aboriginal rights in order to deny them.

In the spring of 1988, Grand Chief Mitchell of the Mohawks of Akwesasne crossed the St. Lawrence River from the United States into Canada at Cornwall, Ontario. He brought with him blankets, bibles, motor oil, clothing and a washing machine to trade with the Mohawks of Tyendinaga. He refused to pay duty on the goods on the basis that he was exercising an Aboriginal right under section 35.

Although he was successful at trial and on appeal, the Supreme Court decided against Grand Chief Mitchell. The Court's grounds for dismissing his claim were twofold. First, the Court rejected Grand Chief Mitchell's position that the right he was exercising was the Mohawks' Aboriginal right to enter Canada from the US with personal and community goods without paying duty and to trade those goods with other First Nations. Instead, the Court described the asserted Aboriginal right as the right to bring goods across the St. Lawrence River for trading purposes.

The Court then decided Grand Chief Mitchell had failed to introduce sufficient evidence at trial to support the existence of this newly described, narrow Aboriginal right. While there was plenty of evidence of the Mohawk trading with other First Nations, especially eastward and westward, little to no specific evidence had been presented at trial to prove the Mohawk had traded northward across the St. Lawrence. The Court held that even if the Mohawk had traded northward across the St. Lawrence, based on the *Van der Peet* test, such trading was "incidental" and not integral to who the Mohawk were as an Indigenous People.

Mitchell exemplifies how the Supreme Court wields its authority to recharacterize Indigenous Peoples' claimed Aboriginal rights to justify denying them. As it had done in *Pamajewon*, the Court rejected Grand Chief Mitchell's description of the right and then, unsurprisingly, decided he had failed to prove a right he hadn't claimed.

Why Is the *Desautel* Decision Important?

Aboriginal Rights – "Aboriginal Peoples" – Purpose of Section 35

The Supreme Court's 2021 Desautel decision is important because it confirmed that Indigenous people who reside outside Canada and are not Canadian citizens may be able to exercise section 35 rights.

When fur trader David Thompson travelled through the Arrow Lakes region of modern-day British Columbia in 1811 he encountered *Nsyilxcən*-speaking Indigenous people. Nearly two hundred years later, Rick Desautel, a descendant of the people Thompson met, shot an elk in the same area. As a United States citizen and non-resident of Canada, Desautel was charged under the provincial Wildlife Act. His defence was that he was exercising an Aboriginal right protected by section 35 of the constitution.

The central question for the Court was whether Indigenous people residing outside Canada can have Aboriginal rights in Canada under section 35 of the constitution.

For a majority of the Court, the answer was "yes." Section 35's reference to the "Aboriginal peoples of Canada," the Court decided, means the modern-day successors of the Indigenous people who, at the time of contact with Europeans, occupied the lands that subsequently became Canada. Their descendants are part of the "Aboriginal peoples of Canada," whether or not they currently reside in Canada or are Canadian citizens.

The trial judge had decided Desautel was a member of an Indigenous group that was a modern-day successor to the *Nsyilxcən*-speaking people Thompson had met in 1811, so the remaining question was whether Desautel was exercising an Aboriginal right. The Court decided this question should be decided based on the existing test for proving an Aboriginal right, and the result was that Desautel was found to be exercising an Aboriginal right when he shot the elk.

The *Desautel* decision left many questions unanswered, including: What test applies to determine whether a Métis community is an "Aboriginal people of Canada"? Are the constitutional rights for Indigenous communities outside Canada different from those within Canada? What is the scope of consultation owed to Indigenous communities outside Canada? What test for Aboriginal title might apply?

Why Is the *C-92* *Reference* Decision Important?

Aboriginal Rights – Self-government

The Supreme Court's 2024 C-92 Reference decision is important because it confirmed Parliament's power to recognize Indigenous Peoples' inherent right to self-government.

The First Nations, Inuit and Métis Children, Youth and Families Act was part of the federal government's fulfillment of its commitments under the United Nations Declaration on the Rights of Indigenous Peoples (UNDRIP) to recognize Indigenous Peoples' self-government rights and responsibility for the upbringing and care of Indigenous children.

The federal legislation allowed for the enforcement of laws First Nations, Inuit and Métis would create to protect their children and provide family services. The legislation was intended to breathe life into Indigenous law-making authority. Quebec challenged the legislation, arguing the federal government could not interfere with the provinces' authority over child and family services.

The Court emphasized that Parliament can pass laws that recognize Indigenous jurisdiction, make this recognition binding on the Crown, and declare that if there's a conflict, the Indigenous law will prevail over other laws. Parliament's power to do this comes from the federal government's constitutional authority over "Indians, and lands reserved for the Indians," i.e. section 91(24) of the constitution (see "Why is the division of powers important?").

The effect of Parliament's recognition of Indigenous Peoples' inherent right of self-government, and that it includes child and family services, protected by section 35 of the constitution, is to make it binding on everyone who represents the Crown. While it's not binding on the courts, it would be very meaningful should the courts ever be called on to decide the issue.

Many commentators have misunderstood the effect of the Court's decision. The Supreme Court did not confirm that Indigenous Peoples have an inherent right of self-government protected by section 35. The Court left that question unanswered.

Importantly, when Indigenous Peoples develop a child and family services law, their law will not be enforced based on a recognition of their inherent rights. Instead, it will be given effect through the federal government's constitutional authority to pass laws in relation to "Indians, and lands reserved for the Indians"—the same power the federal government uses to impose the Indian Act on Indigenous people.

TREATY RIGHTS

Why Is the *Nowegijick* Decision Important?

Treaties – Interpretation – Legislation

The Supreme Court's 1983 Nowegijick *decision is important because it established the legal principle that uncertainties in treaties or laws relating to Indigenous people should be decided in favour of Indigenous people.*

Section 87 of the Indian Act exempts from taxation a status Indian's personal property if the property is situated on reserve. Gene Nowegijick, a member of Gull Bay First Nation, argued that based on section 87 he didn't have to pay income tax on money he made working as a logger for the First Nation's development corporation.

The debate at the Court was whether Nowegijick's taxable income was "personal property" under section 87 of the Indian Act or simply a dollar amount arrived at through the Income Tax Act.

The general rule is that tax exemptions only apply when they are clear and unambiguous. In *Nowegijick*, the Court decided that when considering laws relating to Indigenous people, including the Indian Act, any uncertainty should be interpreted in favour of Indigenous people. This became known as the *Nowegijick* **principle**.

Instead of a technical, legalistic approach, the Court said it was important to give effect to the plain ordinary meaning of the language as it would be understood by Indigenous people.

Nowegijick continues to be relied on at all levels of court, though more recent decisions have stressed that a liberal, generous interpretation can't go so far as to stretch the meaning of a law or treaty beyond what is reasonable (see "Why are the *Marshall* decisions important?").

Why Is the *Simon* Decision Important?

Treaty Rights – Incidental Rights

The Supreme Court's 1985 Simon *decision is important because it confirmed the Peace and Friendship Treaties in the Maritimes are the source of treaty rights.*

In 1980 Jim Simon, a member of the Sipekne'katik First Nation, was charged under Nova Scotia's legislation with possession of a rifle and shotgun during a closed hunting season.

At trial, Simon argued that the Peace and Friendship Treaty of 1752 between the British and the Mi'kmaq had guaranteed the Mi'kmaq the right to hunt and that the right could not be interfered with by the Province.

The Court rejected the argument from the 1929 *Syliboy* decision that the Treaty of 1752 was not a valid treaty because the Mi'kmaq were "savages" and so had lacked the capacity to enter into a treaty with the British. The Court also rejected the argument that if the Treaty of 1752 had in fact been a legitimate treaty, it had been terminated in 1753 when the Mi'kmaq and the British had resumed hostilities.

The Court clarified that Simon's possession of the rifle and the shotgun was part and parcel of exercising the treaty right.

In the end, Simon was acquitted on both charges on the basis that provincial legislation could not stop him from carrying the rifle and the shotgun because under section 88 of the Indian Act, the Province could not interfere with the hunting right guaranteed under the Treaty of 1752.

The *Simon* decision set the groundwork for the later *Marshall* decision, which established the Mi'kmaq treaty right to a commercial fishery. Following the *Simon* decision, Mi'kmaq Treaty Day began to be celebrated every October 1.

Why Is the *Horseman* Decision Important?

Treaty Rights – Natural Resources Transfer Agreement

The Supreme Court's 1990 Horseman *decision is important because the Supreme Court allowed Canada to break its promise to protect the Treaty 8 commercial hunting right.*

Bert Horseman, a member of Horse Lake First Nation, shot a grizzly bear in self-defence. A year later, unemployed and living on his reserve, he sold the bearskin to raise money to feed his family. He was found guilty under the Alberta Wildlife Act for trafficking in wildlife.

In a four-to-three decision, the Supreme Court upheld Horseman's conviction. It decided that although Canada had promised Treaty 8 Indigenous people in 1899 that they could continue their traditional economy based in part on hunting for commercial purposes, in 1930 Canada unilaterally extinguished Treaty 8 commercial hunting when it transferred so-called Crown lands to Alberta through the Natural Resources Transfer Agreement in 1930. All that remained was the right to hunt for food (see "Why are the Natural Resources Transfer Agreements Important?").

From the day of its release in 1990, the *Horseman* decision has been roundly criticized. The three dissenting justices identified the contradiction between the Court describing treaties as solemn agreements, but then endorsing the federal government's bad faith in reneging on the Crown's promises. For prairie treaty First Nations, *Horseman* continues to exemplify the Crown's broken promises and the hollowness of the Supreme Court's assurances that treaties must be respected.

Why Is the *Sioui* Decision Important?

Treaty Rights – Requirements for Treaty

The Supreme Court's 1990 Sioui decision is important because it was part of the development of modern treaty interpretation principles.

In the spring of 1982 four members of the Huron-Wendat Nation from the Wendake community near Quebec City were charged under a provincial law for cutting down trees, making fires and camping in Jacques-Cartier National Park. In their defence, they argued they were exercising treaty rights.

The Court considered whether a one-paragraph document signed by General James Murray on September 5, 1760, confirming the Huron-Wendat's right to "the free exercise of their religion, their customs and liberty of trading with the English," was a treaty.

The Court confirmed that the document had to be understood based on a consideration of historical context and the common understanding of the British and the Huron-Wendat in 1760.

The Court decided it was reasonable for the Huron-Wendat to have assumed General Murray had the authority on behalf of the British to enter into a treaty since he had a history of representing the Crown in important matters. The central question was whether there was evidence Murray and the Huron-Wendat intended to create mutually binding obligations. A certain degree of solemnity shortly after the agreement was made was evidence it was intended to be a treaty.

Based on all the circumstances and the historical context, the Court decided the document was a treaty and that the Huron-Wendat were not guilty because they were exercising treaty rights. *Sioui* continues to be relied on as a fundamental decision in the interpretation of treaty rights (see "Why Is the Supreme Court's *Restoule* Decision Important?").

Why Is the *Badger* Decision Important?

Treaty Rights – Infringement – Natural Resources Transfer Agreement

The Supreme Court's 1996 Badger decision is important because it confirmed the Crown must justify treaty infringements based on the test developed for infringements of Aboriginal rights.

Three Treaty 8 First Nation men hunted moose for food on privately owned lands. They were charged under the Alberta Wildlife Act for either hunting out of season or without a licence.

The Supreme Court emphasized that historical treaties between the Crown and Indigenous people were oral agreements. The written treaty document did not always record the full extent of the treaty. Therefore, treaties should be interpreted based on Indigenous people's understanding at the time of the oral agreement. According to the Court, the primary objective of Indigenous people when Treaty 8 was agreed to in 1899 was to ensure they could continue to pursue their livelihood as hunters, trappers and fishers.

The Court endorsed principles established by lower courts that the honour of the Crown is always at stake when governments deal with Indigenous people and no appearance of sharp dealing will be sanctioned.

While the Natural Resources Transfer Agreement of 1930 (see "Why are the Natural Resources Transfer Agreements Important?") had modified the treaty right by extinguishing its commercial aspect, the Crown still had to justify any infringement. The Court concluded that the remaining treaty right included a right of access to private lands to hunt for food if the land was unoccupied and not put to a use visibly incompatible with hunting, e.g. a farmyard. The Court dismissed the appeals of two of the First Nation men. For the third man, the Court ordered a new trial to determine whether the government had justified the infringement of the treaty right.

Badger is a stark example of cognitive dissonance at play in the Supreme Court's formative section 35 decisions. In one breath it could describe treaties as solemn agreements, caution against sharp dealing and lecture on the honour of the Crown, yet still approve the Crown's breaking of treaty promises.

Why Is the *Sundown* Decision Important?

Treaty Rights – Incidental Rights

The Supreme Court's 1999 Sundown *decision is important because it clarified what rights are incidental to recognized Aboriginal and treaty rights.*

In 1992, John Sundown, a member of Big Island Cree Nation, was charged under provincial law for building a cabin in Saskatchewan's Meadow Lake Provincial Park. In defence, Sundown argued his First Nation's Treaty 6 hunting right included the right to build a hunting cabin in the park.

There was no question that Sundown had the right to hunt in the park. The issue at the Supreme Court was whether building the hunting cabin was "reasonably incidental" to exercising the hunting right. The Court decided that to determine whether an activity is reasonably incidental to a hunting or fishing right the question is: would a reasonable person, fully apprised of the relevant manner of hunting or fishing, consider the activity in question reasonably related to the act of hunting or fishing?

The Court concluded Big Island Cree Nation members had historically hunted by building a base camp from which they would make hunting trips, returning each night to the camp for shelter and to dress the day's kill. Sundown's cabin was a modern-day equivalent of this practice that existed at the time Big Island Cree Nation entered into Treaty 6. Therefore, the cabin was permitted because it was incidental to exercising the Treaty 6 hunting right.

The *Sundown* decision continues to be important for First Nations across Canada when their members face indirect attacks on their established rights through the imposition of federal or provincial regulations.

Why Are the *Marshall* Decisions Important?

Treaty Rights – Commercial Rights – Regulation

The Supreme Court's 1999 Marshall *decisions are important because they recognized a Mi'kmaq treaty right to a commercial fishery.*

In the summer of 1993, after being imprisoned for twelve years on a wrongful murder conviction, Donald Marshall Jr. sold 463 pounds of eels he and a friend had caught near Pomquet Harbour, Nova Scotia. His defence to charges of illegal fishing was that he was exercising a treaty right promised to the Mi'kmaq by the British in 1760.

To determine whether a treaty right existed, the Court examined the wording and circumstances of the Peace and Friendship Treaty entered into at Halifax on March 10, 1760, by the Mi'kmaq and British Governor Charles Lawrence. The Mi'kmaq made a series of promises, including to not assist the French or attack the British, and to release British prisoners. The Mi'kmaq also promised to not barter or trade goods except at "truck houses" (trading posts) established by the British. The question for the Court was whether this promise was the basis for a modern-day right to a commercial fishery. The majority of judges decided it was.

Their conclusion was based on going beyond the written document and considering evidence of why the Mi'kmaq and British made the treaty. In doing so, the Court confirmed an important treaty interpretation principle: it would be unconscionable for the Crown to rely on the written terms of a treaty while ignoring the oral terms.

The Court had to consider that recognizing a Mi'kmaq treaty right to a commercial fishery could lead to the Mi'kmaq catching all the available fish with factory trawlers, leaving none for non-Indigenous commercial fishers. It addressed this concern by limiting the treaty fishing right to catching enough to support a "moderate livelihood" (see "Why Is the *Gladstone* Decision Important?"), relying on the language in the treaty that described the truck house as being intended to provide the Mi'kmaq with "necessaries." The Court described a moderate livelihood as enough money to pay for day-to-day needs including food, clothing, housing and a few amenities but not the accumulation of wealth.

The Court's confirmation of the Mi'kmaq commercial fishing treaty right ignited a backlash in the fall of 1999 led by non-Indigenous commercial fishers. As a result, the Court took the unusual step of issuing a second set of reasons confirming the federal government's authority to regulate the Mi'kmaq commercial fishery.

Marshall is an example of how even when Indigenous people win at the Supreme Court, they are still reliant on governments to honourably implement the decision. More than twenty-five years after the *Marshall* decisions, the Mi'kmaq are still fighting to have their commercial fishery treaty right respected by the federal government.

Why Is the *Grassy Narrows* Decision Important?

Treaty Rights – Infringement

The Supreme Court's 2014 Grassy Narrows *decision is important because it opened the door for provincial governments to infringe treaty rights.*

Grassy Narrows First Nation opposed Ontario's granting of a forestry licence to a large forestry company. It argued the licence infringed its treaty rights guaranteed under Treaty 3 and that, as a provincial government, Ontario did not have the authority to infringe rights protected by section 35.

Similar to many of the so-called historic treaties, Treaty 3 includes a clause allowing the Crown to "take up" lands from time to time for settlement, mining, forestry and other purposes. The question for the Court was whether Ontario could exercise this clause unilaterally, or whether Canada has to be involved.

The question raised an important issue for many First Nations across Canada who understand their treaty relationship to be with the British Crown. They might reluctantly accept the federal government as the Crown's modern-day representative, but they vigorously reject the suggestion that a provincial government is their treaty partner (see "Aren't the Treaties with the King?").

The Supreme Court saw the treaty relationship differently. Even though Ontario played no part in negotiating Treaty 3 in 1873, the Court decided that under Canadian law the Province is both bound by the treaty and can rely on its provisions to take up lands for various purposes without the involvement of the federal government. The Court explained that Treaty 3 was made between the Anishinaabe of Treaty 3 and the Crown and under Canadian law, Ontario is just as much the Crown as Canada.

Grassy Narrows represented a radical about-face for the Court. Just eight years earlier in the *Morris* decision, another treaty case, it flatly rejected the argument that provincial governments could infringe treaty rights. In *Grassy Narrows*, relying on the *Tsilhqot'in* Aboriginal title decision, but without explanation, it reversed its position and opened the door for provincial governments to override treaty rights.

Why Is the *Shot Both Sides* Decision Important?

Treaty Rights – Limitation Periods – Declarations

The Supreme Court's 2024 Shot Both Sides *decision is important because it is an example of the Court's increasing reliance on outcomes that do not force the Crown to do anything specific to make good on a broken promise to First Nations.*

When the Blood Tribe in modern-day southern Alberta entered into Treaty 7 with the Crown in 1877, it was promised one square mile of land for each family of five. Canada failed to fulfill the promise. There was a shortfall of more than 162 square miles of land set aside. The Blood Tribe asked the Court to order Canada to provide the outstanding lands and pay compensation for loss of use.

In most situations, anyone with a legal claim against someone else must file the claim in court within the time period specified in a provincial or federal law—often six years. The time limit is called a limitation period. If they fail to do so, the party they sue can argue that because the claimant took too long to bring their claim to court, the judge cannot award them compensation.

Although the Blood Tribe was aware as early as 1971 that it had the basis for a lawsuit against Canada, its claim wasn't filed in court until 1980. While Canada admitted breaking its treaty promise, it argued the claim was filed beyond the six-year time limit. The Blood Tribe argued that although its claim was filed in 1980, First Nations couldn't successfully pursue a claim based on treaty rights until 1982 when treaty rights were granted protection under section 35 of the constitution.

The Court rejected the Blood Tribe's argument because it is well established that treaty rights could be enforced in the courts from the date of treaty. Although section 35 of the constitution protects existing rights, it did not create rights or make existing rights legally enforceable.

The Court did grant the Blood Tribe a declaration that in failing to fulfill the treaty promise, Canada had breached the honour of the Crown. The declaration does not force Canada to do anything specific, but the Court hoped that it would encourage Canada to resolve the Blood Tribe's claim through good faith negotiations.

Why Is the Supreme Court's *Restoule* Decision Important?

Treaty Rights

The Supreme Court's 2024 Restoule *decision is important because it exemplifies how the Court uses the rhetoric of moral outrage to mask its undermining of treaty promises.*

In 1850 the Crown entered into two treaties with the Anishinaabe of the Upper Great Lakes region of Ontario. Although the so-called Robinson Treaties promised annual payments to the Anishinaabe would increase, they had remained frozen at $4 per person since 1875.

The Anishinaabe sued the provincial and federal governments for breach of treaty and sought billions of dollars in compensation. After being largely successful at trial and the Ontario Court of Appeal, the Robinson-Huron treaty First Nations settled for $10 billion. The Robinson-Superior treaty First Nations did not settle with Canada and Ontario, so the matter proceeded to the Supreme Court.

Given the annuity was still paid out at the 1875 amount of $4, the Court concluded that it was obvious it needed to be increased and that the Crown owed the Anishinaabe past compensation. It ordered the Crown to try to negotiate a settlement with Robinson-Superior treaty First Nations. If a settlement was not reached within six months, the Crown had to make a settlement offer which the trial judge could review and, if justified, substitute with her own decision on a settlement amount.

While the Supreme Court agreed with the trial judge that the Crown had breached its treaty promise to the Anishinaabe, it substituted its own description of the promise to water down the Crown's obligation. Instead of a mandatory obligation to increase annuity payments, the

Supreme Court decided the Crown's promise was to consider, from time to time, whether it could increase the annuity without losing money and if it could, to decide whether or not to increase it and by how much.

Unlike the trial judge or the Court of Appeal, the Supreme Court introduced new factors for the Crown to consider when deciding whether and by how much to increase the annuity, including the number of treaty beneficiaries and their needs and the wider needs of Indigenous and non-Indigenous people in Ontario and across Canada. These factors, which have no basis in the agreement negotiated by the Anishinaabe in 1850, favour Canada and Ontario and potentially undermine the value of the treaty promise.

For treaty First Nations, *Restoule* exemplifies two troubling, persistent patterns in the Supreme Court's consideration of treaties: its baseless description of treaties as land surrender agreements, and its eagerness to express moral outrage while imposing its own interpretation of treaties, which either denies the existence of treaty promises or undermines their value for First Nations.

FIDUCIARY DUTY

Why Is the *Guerin* Decision Important?

Fiduciary Duty – Reserve Lands

The Supreme Court's 1984 Guerin decision is important because it established the principle that in certain situations the Crown must act in the best interests of Indigenous people and if it fails to do so it can be sued in court.

The Musqueam Indian Band sued Canada after it discovered the terms of a lease the federal government had negotiated with a golf club for part of its Vancouver-area reserve were less favourable than it had been led to believe.

The main issue in *Guerin* was whether Indigenous people could take the federal government to court for failing to act in their best interest. The Court concluded that when the Crown takes responsibility for deciding what is in the best interest of Indigenous people, it has a legal obligation to act in their best interest—this is referred to as a fiduciary duty. If the Crown fails in this duty, it can be sued in court.

Guerin is one of the most important cases decided by the Supreme Court because for the first time, the federal government was held legally responsible for not acting in the best interest of Indigenous people.

Why Is the *Osoyoos* Decision Important?

Expropriation of Reserve Lands – Taxation

The Supreme Court's 2001 Osoyoos decision is important because it confirmed the principle of minimal impairment applies when the Crown expropriates Indian Act reserve land.

In the 1920s a canal was constructed through the Osoyoos Indian Band's reserve to provide water for farms and orchards developed by World War I veterans. The expropriation of the band's reserve lands as a right-of-way for the irrigation canal was confirmed through a 1957 federal order-in-council. In the 1990s, the band sought to apply its Indian Act tax bylaw to the expropriated land. The Town of Oliver disputed the tax bill, arguing the expropriated lands were no longer "in the reserve" and therefore the band's tax bylaw did not apply.

The principal debate at the Court was about whether the Court's principles on Aboriginal title applied to the expropriation of Indian Act reserve land. The minority of the Court decided they did not—the established law of expropriation should apply, just as it would off reserve. Consequently, the band's full interest in the land was expropriated and the band could not enforce its tax bylaw.

The majority of judges disagreed. They reasoned that while reserve lands are not identical to Aboriginal title lands, neither are they equivalent to off-reserve, fee simple lands. Unlike when it expropriates fee simple land, when the Crown expropriates reserve lands its fiduciary duty to Indigenous people is triggered. As a result, if the Crown intends to take a full interest in reserve land, its intention must be clear and plain. Also, instead of taking the full interest in the land, it will be assumed that the Crown will take no more than required to achieve the purpose of an expropriation.

Applying these principles, the majority of the Court decided that because it was not clear and plain that the Crown intended to expropriate the band's full interest in its reserve lands and because the right-of-way for the irrigation canal did not require the expropriation of the band's full interest, the land was still "in the reserve" for the purposes of the band's tax bylaw.

Because of the narrow win in *Osoyoos*, the federal government is held to a higher standard when dealing with reserve land across Canada.

Why Is the *Wewaykum* Decision Important?

Fiduciary Duty – Reserve Creation

The Supreme Court's 2002 Wewaykum *decision is important because it narrowed the scope of the Crown's fiduciary duty to Indigenous people.*

We Wai Kai Nation (Cape Mudge Band) and Wei Wai Kum First Nation (Campbell River Indian Band) each claimed the other's reserve on Vancouver Island. Instead of displacing their neighbour from their reserve land, they sought damages from Canada for its failure to properly set aside reserves for each Nation's sole benefit.

Following the 1984 *Guerin* decision, the courts were inundated with fiduciary duty claims. In *Wewaykum*, the Court sought to stem the flood by clarifying that the existence of a fiduciary relationship between the Crown and Indigenous people does not mean every aspect of that relationship results in a fiduciary duty.

Even if a fiduciary duty does exist, the Crown's responsibilities vary depending on the circumstances. For example, when the Crown is in the process of setting aside reserve lands, but the reserve has not yet been confirmed, the Crown's responsibilities include loyalty, good faith, full disclosure of information and acting with ordinary diligence and prudence to protect the best interests of the First Nation. Once the reserve is officially created, the Crown's fiduciary duty expands to include protecting and preserving a First Nation's interests in its reserve lands. If a First Nation were to later surrender reserve lands, the Crown's fiduciary duty includes ordinary diligence to prevent exploitive bargains.

The Court decided that despite the long history of reserve creation in BC, reserves were not officially created until administration and control of reserve lands were transferred to the federal government in

1938. During the preceding years, Canada had not breached its limited fiduciary duty to either First Nation, so their claims could not succeed. *Wewaykum* was a major part of the Supreme Court's efforts, post *Guerin*, to put a brake on First Nations holding the federal government accountable for breach of fiduciary duty.

Why Is the *Williams Lake* Decision Important?

Fiduciary Duty – Specific Claims

The Supreme Court's 2018 Williams Lake *decision is important because it upheld the authority of the Specific Claims Tribunal and established that Canada can be held liable for the actions of colonial governments.*

First Nations are unable to seek justice for many of Canada's historic wrongs because of time limits on filing claims in court. An alternative is to file a specific claim against Canada in the hope Canada will agree to negotiate a settlement. If Canada rejects the claim, First Nations can bring it to the Specific Claims Tribunal for an independent decision. Williams Lake followed this process in the hopes of receiving compensation for the loss of its traditional village site.

Contrary to colonial law against the preemption of "Indian settlements," the Williams Lake First Nation's village site was pre-empted before British Columbia joined Canada as a province in 1871. In the 1880s the Indian Reserve Commissioner refused to cancel the pre-emptions and instead assigned the First Nation a reserve in a different location. The First Nation filed a specific claim for the taking of its village site. The Specific Claims Tribunal decided the First Nation's claim was valid but the Federal Court of Appeal dismissed the claim. Williams Lake appealed to the Supreme Court.

The Court agreed with the tribunal that at the time of the pre-emption, the First Nation had an interest in the land based on its historic use and occupation as a village site. This interest gave rise to the Crown's fiduciary duty to act in good faith and with ordinary good judgment to protect the First Nation's interests. Following British Columbia's entry into Confederation in 1871, Canada assumed the fiduciary role of the exclusive middleman between the Province and First Nations when it came to reserve creation.

Following Confederation, the Indian Reserve Commissioner chose not to cancel the pre-emptions and Canada failed to intervene to protect the First Nation's interests. As a result, the Crown breached its fiduciary duty. The setting aside of different lands for a reserve for the First Nation did not excuse the breach. Therefore, the First Nation's claim was valid.

The Specific Claims Tribunal was established in response to First Nation demands for an independent body to assess their specific claims. The *Williams Lake* decision was important for confirming that the tribunal's processes and decisions deserve respect from the courts.

Why Is the *Southwind* Decision Important?

Fiduciary Duty – Compensation – Specific Claims

The Supreme Court's 2021 Southwind *decision is important because it clarified the principles for calculating compensation when Canada breaches a fiduciary duty to a First Nation.*

In 1928 Canada, Ontario and Manitoba decided to build a dam on Lac Seul in northwestern Ontario to generate hydroelectricity for Winnipeg. Affected non-Indigenous people and organizations, including the Anglican Church, were compensated for damages from the flooding. Lac Seul First Nation, whose reserve bordered the lake, received nothing, despite the flooding all but ruining its reserve. While the trial judge and Federal Court of Appeal decided Canada had breached its fiduciary duty to Lac Seul and awarded damages of $30 million, the First Nation appealed to the Supreme Court arguing the compensation was insufficient.

The Supreme Court decided the courts below had not applied the correct principles when calculating compensation for Canada's breach of its fiduciary duty to Lac Seul and ordered a new trial.

The Court rejected Canada's argument that the value of the compensation should not be more than what Lac Seul would have received if Canada had not breached its fiduciary duty and simply expropriated the land. This is because compensation is intended, in part, to deter Canada from breaching fiduciary duties to First Nations in the future. Therefore, the trial judge should have calculated compensation based on the highest and best use of the land, which in this case was hydroelectricity generation.

Southwind reset the basis for calculating compensation for breach of the Crown's fiduciary duty to First Nations. For decades, the federal government had increasingly taken an ungenerous and self-serving position on calculating compensation. In *Southwind* the Court restated fundamental principles laid down in *Guerin*. It also confirmed that Canada's failure to negotiate the best deal possible for a First Nation can be a breach of its fiduciary duty.

Following the *Southwind* decision, Canada and Lac Seul negotiated a settlement that included $234 million in compensation.

DUTY TO CONSULT
AND ACCOMMODATE

Why Is the *Haida* Decision Important?

Aboriginal Rights – Duty to Consult

The Supreme Court's 2004 Haida *decision is important because it established the Crown's constitutional obligation to consult and accommodate Indigenous peoples with unrecognized Aboriginal rights.*

The Haida Nation had longstanding concerns about the effects of logging on their Aboriginal title and rights. They opposed the British Columbia provincial government's replacement and transfer of a tree farm licence that allowed a large forestry company to log trees on Haida Gwaii. The Court had to decide what legal obligations, if any, the Crown owes Indigenous people when governments consider making a decision that will affect "asserted" Aboriginal rights, i.e. rights denied by the Crown.

Governments and industry argued there was no need to impose new legal obligations on the Crown. Instead, Indigenous people could either go to court to have their rights confirmed or they could ask a court for an injunction to prevent the government from making the decision until their rights were proven in court. The Court rejected these options as impractical because of the time and expense of proving Aboriginal rights in court, and because Indigenous people had little chance of getting an injunction against government and industry based on their unrecognized Aboriginal rights.

The Court decided it would not uphold the honour of the Crown to unilaterally allow governments to authorize activities that would harm Aboriginal rights while the possible recognition of those rights dragged on through negotiations or the courts. Consequently, the Court concluded that when the Crown is aware of an asserted Aboriginal right and the possibility that its conduct or decision will harm the Aboriginal right, it has a legal obligation to consult and possibly accommodate Indigenous people. The level of consultation owed depends on the strength of the claim to the Aboriginal right and the potential harmful effect on the right. The stronger the claim and more serious the effect, the greater the level of consultation, and possible accommodation, owed by the Crown. The Court decided that the Province had failed to fulfill the Crown's duty to consult and accommodate the Haida.

The *Haida* decision was the most important Aboriginal law decision since the *Delgamuukw* decision in 1997. It forced governments and industry across Canada to take Indigenous concerns seriously or otherwise risk delays or even cancellations of their projects.

Why Is the *Taku* Decision Important?

Aboriginal Rights – Duty to Consult

The Supreme Court's 2004 Taku decision is important because it created modest requirements for the Crown to fulfill the duty to consult.

The Taku River Tlingit First Nation opposed the reopening of a mine in its territory in northwestern British Columbia. The proposed access road was of particular concern for Taku River. The Province conducted an environmental assessment and, over the First Nation's objections, approved the project. Taku River challenged the approval in court, arguing the Province had failed to properly consult and accommodate it before making the decision.

The Supreme Court heard the *Taku* and *Haida* appeals at the same time. The general principles explained in *Haida* were applied in *Taku* in the context of a provincial environmental assessment.

Given the Taku River's strength of claim to title and rights and the serious potential effects of the mine, especially the access road, the Court decided the Province owed Taku River more than minimal consultation and that some form of accommodation was required. In contrast to the *Haida* decision, however, the Court decided the Province had fulfilled its responsibility to consult and accommodate Taku River.

Of importance to the Court was that the environmental assessment had lasted for three and a half years. Taku River had directly participated in the environmental assessment. The final approval included provisions to address some of Taku River's concerns. Although Taku River was unsatisfied with the accommodation measures, the Court stressed that the Province was not obligated to reach an agreement with Taku River.

The *Taku* decision significantly undermined the *Haida* decision's potential to meaningfully address Indigenous concerns. It confirmed that the Crown can rely on project proponents and its own processes designed for other purposes as part of fulfilling the duty to consult and accommodate. Most importantly, *Taku* confirmed Indigenous people are entitled to a process based on the duty to consult, but not to any particular outcome; there is no requirement for the process to be any more than adequate. Future court decisions, relying on *Taku*, have demonstrated that provincial and federal governments gradually became more sophisticated in providing Indigenous people with the bare minimum to meet the duty to consult.

Why Is the *Mikisew I* Decision Important?

Treaty Rights – Duty to Consult – Infringement

The Supreme Court's 2005 Mikisew I decision is important because it established that governments have to consult First Nations when they intend to put treaty lands to different purposes, and if too much land is made unavailable for exercising treaty rights, First Nations can sue for treaty infringement.

The federal government approved a new winter road in Wood Buffalo National Park in Alberta that would run alongside Mikisew Cree First Nation's reserve. Mikisew opposed the road because of how it would affect their harvesting rights guaranteed under Treaty 8.

The Court emphasized that treaties were not intended to finalize the relationship between Indigenous and non-Indigenous people. Instead, treaties should establish principles for an ongoing relationship that requires care and respect from all government officials. The Court rejected the argument that every government decision that affects a treaty right is an infringement of the right. Instead, when a treaty specifically contemplates that lands will be used for different purposes (mining, forestry, settlement, etc.) the Crown's obligation can be met through the duty to consult and accommodate, i.e. the same requirement as for unrecognized Aboriginal rights.

The Court also rejected the argument that lands in a First Nation's traditional territory could be taken up for different purposes without infringing the treaty so long as members could exercise their treaty rights somewhere in the province. Instead, if so much of a First Nation's territory is used for various purposes that they no longer have a meaningful opportunity to exercise their treaty rights, they can sue the government for infringing their treaty.

The Court cancelled the decision authorizing the winter road. Consultation was flawed from the outset because the government never intended to meaningfully address Mikisew's concerns. Following the *Mikisew* decision there was uncertainty about the tipping point for treaty infringement—does it only occur when there is no meaningful ability left to exercise treaty rights, or does it occur sometime before? In the *Saik'uz* decision (see page 200), the Court decided it is when treaty rights have been significantly diminished.

Why Is the *Rio Tinto* Decision Important?

Duty to Consult – Administrative Tribunals – Trigger for Consultation

The Supreme Court's 2010 Rio Tinto *decision is important because it clarified when tribunals are responsible for the duty to consult and when the duty is triggered.*

In the 1950s, with the approval of the provincial government, Alcan built a dam on the Nechako River, reversing its flow in order to generate hydroelectricity for its aluminum smelter on the British Columbia coast. There was no consultation with affected First Nations. In 2007 BC Hydro signed a contract to buy excess hydroelectricity from Alcan. The contract had to be approved by the British Columbia Utilities Commission, an independent provincial tribunal. The Carrier Sekani Tribal Council argued the commission could not approve the contract without ensuring that the Crown's duty to consult was fulfilled.

Provincial and federal governments often pass legislation that delegates decisions to independent tribunals. The question for the Court was whether these tribunals have a role in fulfilling the Crown's duty to consult and accommodate Indigenous people. The Court decided a tribunal's consultation responsibilities depend on what powers government assigns it—these might range from a tribunal having no responsibility, to a tribunal being responsible for consulting directly, to a tribunal only deciding whether consultation was adequate.

A tribunal is responsible for deciding the adequacy of consultation if it has the power to consider constitutional issues, unless a government specifically limits its responsibility. But a tribunal can only become directly involved in consultation if it has the power to accommodate Indigenous concerns.

On the question of when the duty to consult is triggered, the Court explained the duty arises when the Crown does something that could cause a new effect on Aboriginal rights. Importantly, this is not limited to new physical, on-the-ground effects. So-called strategic level decisions, e.g. transferring or renewing a licence, can by themselves trigger the duty to consult even if there are no new physical effects.

The Court decided that in this case the Utilities Commission had the authority to consider whether consultation was adequate, but did not have the power to enter directly into consultation. It concluded that the tribunal was not unreasonable in deciding that the hydroelectricity purchase agreement would not have any new effect and so the duty to consult was not triggered. Unfortunately, many companies continue to misrepresent *Rio Tinto* by arguing that the duty to consult is triggered only if there are new physical, on-the-ground effects.

Why Is the *Beckman* Decision Important?

Duty to Consult – Modern Treaties

The Supreme Court's 2010 Beckman *decision is important because it confirmed that an independent duty to consult First Nations can exist separately from the terms of a modern-day treaty.*

In 1993, after twenty years of negotiations, Yukon First Nations, Canada and Yukon signed an umbrella agreement that set the basis for subsequent modern-day treaties with individual First Nations. Little Salmon/Carmacks First Nation finalized its treaty in 1996. Settlement lands were confirmed for the First Nation as well as the right to hunt and fish throughout its traditional territory.

The First Nation challenged a 2004 decision by the Yukon government to grant an individual sixty-five hectares of its traditional territory bordering on its settlement lands, arguing a lack of consultation. Yukon's position was that because there was nothing in the treaty about consulting the First Nation about land grants that affected its harvesting rights, there was no obligation to consult on the decision.

The Court emphasized that modern treaties are more than simple contracts; they are about establishing an ongoing relationship. In contrast to historical treaties, modern treaties set out in detail consultation procedures for future decisions. But it does not follow that when a modern treaty is silent on consultation requirements, there is no duty to consult. The duty to consult exists as a matter of law, regardless of whether it is provided for in a treaty.

The Court reviewed the circumstances around the particular land grant and decided that even though Yukon hadn't acknowledged an obligation to consult the First Nation, it had done so adequately and its decision wasn't unreasonable. The *Beckman* decision remains important for the principle that because the Crown's obligations to Indigenous people are constitutional, the Crown can never relieve itself of those obligations through a negotiated agreement.

Why Is the *Behn* Decision Important?

Duty to Consult – Treaty Infringement – Individuals

The Supreme Court's 2013 Behn *decision is important because it raised the possibility that individual community members might be able to file a lawsuit based on the infringement of Aboriginal and treaty rights.*

Members of the Behn (pronounced "Bain") family of the Fort Nelson First Nation in Treaty 8 opposed logging activities on lands their family had long used for hunting and trapping. They constructed a camp to prevent a logging company's access. The company filed a lawsuit against them for interfering with its operations. In defence, the Behns argued the company's permits were invalid because they infringed their treaty rights and there had been a lack of consultation.

Under Canadian law, Aboriginal rights and treaty rights are collective rights. While they are most often exercised by individual community members, e.g. a treaty hunting right, they are held by the Indigenous Nation as a whole. In *Behn*, the Court had to consider whether individual community members could raise legal arguments based on the infringement of treaty rights or the duty to consult, or whether only the representatives of the larger collective (usually Chief and Council) could make those arguments.

The Court explained that an Indigenous Nation can authorize an individual or organization to represent it in order to ensure the Crown's duty to consult and accommodate is fulfilled. But because there was no clear evidence Fort Nelson First Nation had authorized the Behns to represent the nation, the Court decided the Behns could not argue in court that there had been a lack of consultation on the logging permits.

The Court concluded that instead of blockading the logging road, the Behns should have challenged the initial logging permits. Having failed to do so, they couldn't now come to court and make arguments based on the infringement of treaty rights because that would be unfair to the logging company, which had relied on the approval of the permits. To allow the Behns to argue their treaty infringement case would, according to the Court, amount to tolerating "self-help remedies." Consequently, the Behns' appeal was dismissed. The *Behn* decision has subsequently been relied on by lower courts to dismiss Indigenous people's arguments based on their own laws as merely being "self-help remedies," such as the *Coastal GasLink Pipeline* decision by the BC Supreme Court in 2019.

Why Is the *Clyde River* Decision Important?

Duty to Consult – Tribunals – Treaty Rights

The Supreme Court's 2017 Clyde River *decision is important because it clarified the requirements of an independent tribunal to fulfill the duty to consult.*

Oil and gas companies applied to the National Energy Board (NEB) for authorization to conduct offshore seismic testing in Baffin Bay and Davis Strait. The Inuit of Clyde River, who have rights under the 1993 Nunavut Land Claims Agreement, a modern treaty, opposed the application because of its potential effects on their harvesting rights. After the NEB approved the project, the Inuit of Clyde River challenged the decision in court.

The NEB, an independent tribunal, was tasked by the federal government with consulting with Clyde River and deciding whether consultation was adequate. The Court explained that in such circumstances, it is important that the Crown explain to Indigenous people that it is relying on the tribunal to fulfill the duty to consult. While a tribunal may have to decide whether a decision is in the public interest, any decision that would breach constitutionally protected rights can never be in the public interest.

Even when governments assign consultation to a tribunal, the Crown is ultimately responsible for ensuring the duty to consult is fulfilled. If a tribunal is unable to fulfill the duty, the Crown has to become involved and in some cases might have to commit to a separate, parallel consultation with Indigenous people. Because the NEB was responsible for making a decision on behalf of the Crown, it had to ensure the duty to consult was fulfilled before the decision was made. If the duty was not fulfilled, it could not make the decision.

The Court cancelled the NEB's approval of the project because it had not fulfilled the Crown's responsibilities to Clyde River. One reason for its failure was that it incorrectly focussed on the environmental effects of the project while it should have specifically considered the potential effects on Clyde River's treaty rights (see "What Role Do Environmental Assessments Play in Fulfilling the Duty to Consult?"). It also failed to provide a forum for Clyde River to meaningfully engage in consultation, in part because there was no participant funding and because in response to its questions Clyde River was provided a nearly 4,000-page technical document, little of which was translated into Inuktitut and which was nearly impossible to download given the slow internet speeds in the hamlet. Despite the Court's warning in *Clyde River* that the duty to consult shouldn't be conflated with environmental assessments, governments continue to make this mistake all across the country.

Why Is the *Chippewas of the Thames* Decision Important?

Duty to Consult – Tribunals – Cumulative Effects

The Supreme Court's 2017 Chippewas of the Thames decision is import-ant because it confirmed that the Crown can rely on independent tri-bunals to fulfill the duty to consult and that the duty to consult may include the cumulative and ongoing effects of existing projects.

The National Energy Board (NEB) considered a proposal to repurpose an existing oil pipeline that had been constructed through the Chippe-was of the Thames traditional territory in the 1970s without the First Nation's consent. The Chippewas of the Thames were worried about increased risk of impacts on their constitutional rights and sought consultation directly with the federal government, but were told the government was relying on the NEB's consultation process. The NEB imposed conditions on the company and approved the project over the First Nation's objections.

The Court explained that it didn't matter that the federal govern-ment had not directly taken part in the NEB's hearing process—the Crown's duty to consult was nonetheless triggered by the decision the NEB was responsible for making. But the Court agreed with the federal government relying on the NEB process to fulfill the Crown's duty to consult as long as the tribunal had the necessary authority to address issues raised by the First Nations.

The Court rejected the First Nation's argument that the NEB couldn't be tasked with both consulting them and also deciding whether con-sultation was adequate. The Court explained that tribunals often wear more than one hat, and doing so doesn't mean they will be biased in their decision-making. While the Court confirmed that the duty to consult is not intended to address historical impacts on Aboriginal rights, once the duty is triggered, cumulative and ongoing impacts may inform the scope of consultation because the existing state of affairs cannot be simply ignored (see "Does the Duty to Consult Include Cumulative Effects?").

The Court explained that when considering what accommodation measures should be imposed to protect Aboriginal rights, it is acceptable to seek a balance between those protections and the interests of the wider public. This balancing, the Court explained, is part and parcel of reconciliation.

While *Chippewas of the Thames* and *Clyde River* helpfully clarified the role of independent tribunals in the duty to consult, they didn't address the wider problem with shoehorning consultation into processes never intended to respect government-to-government relationships.

Why Is the *Mikisew II* Decision Important?

Treaty Rights – Duty to Consult – Legislation

The Supreme Court's 2018 Mikisew II *decision is important because it established that governments do not have to consult on proposed legislation, but once it becomes law the legislation can be challenged for infringing section 35 rights.*

Mikisew Cree First Nation was concerned that proposed changes to federal environmental assessment laws would affect their treaty rights. They asked the Court to strike down the new laws because the government had not fulfilled its duty to consult when the legislation was in draft.

The majority of the Supreme Court decided the process of making laws does not trigger the duty to consult. The justices explained that law-making is not a Crown decision equivalent to the type of Crown decisions that trigger the duty to consult, e.g. approving a forestry plan or building a road. Instead, law-making is carried out democratically by Parliament or a provincial legislature, separate from the authority of cabinet. When cabinet ministers develop and introduce proposed legislation, they are acting in their capacity as individual members of the legislature, not as decision-makers in cabinet. It is important, the Court decided, that the law-making process not be subject to oversight by the courts; instead, the courts can only become involved after a proposed bill becomes law.

In response to concerns that if the duty to consult does not apply to law-making, laws could be introduced or changed that would effectively allow governments to act arbitrarily and ignore either asserted or recognized Aboriginal rights, the justices explained that other remedies might be available. For example, if a new law infringes recognized rights, it could then be challenged and a lack of consultation during the development of the law would undermine any argument that the law was justified.

Ultimately, *Mikisew II* is still about Indigenous people hoping to influence the development of colonizers' laws that affect them. The focus needs to shift to creating space for recognizing Indigenous Peoples' own laws.

MÉTIS RIGHTS

Why Is the *Powley* Decision Important?

Métis – Section 35 – Aboriginal Rights

The Supreme Court's 2003 Powley *decision is important because it established the test for recognizing Métis rights under section 35.*

In the fall of 1993, Steve Powley and his son Roddy shot a moose a little north of Sault Ste. Marie, Ontario. They were charged by provincial conservation officers for hunting without a licence. Their defence was that as Métis, they had a section 35 right to hunt for food.

Section 35 of the constitution protects the Aboriginal rights of "Indian, Inuit and Métis peoples of Canada." For the first time the Supreme Court had to consider how to identify the Métis for the purpose of exercising Aboriginal rights under section 35. The Court stressed that "Métis" in section 35 does not refer to all people of mixed European and Indigenous ancestry. Instead, it includes people of mixed ancestry in a specific geographic area whose ancestors had their own separate and distinct shared customs, traditions, way of life and collective identity prior to the establishment of European control in their particular part of Canada.

As with other section 35 rights, Métis rights are limited to a specific location—they are not free-floating rights throughout the country or a province. The Court captured this limitation in its description of the right claimed by the Powleys—it was the right to hunt for food in the area of Sault Ste. Marie. The Powleys had to prove that their ancestors were part of the historic Métis community that existed in the Sault Ste. Marie area.

While the Court did not create a strict test for identifying Métis under section 35, it did set out three general requirements: self-identification, ancestral connection and community acceptance. The Powleys were successful in court, but the requirements for proving Métis rights under section 35 developed in their case have proven difficult for others to meet. While many people of mixed ancestry might self-identify as Métis and be accepted by a modern-day Métis community, they must also prove the existence over one hundred years ago of a historic Métis community in the specific location they are seeking to exercise rights. They must also prove their ancestors were part of that historic community (see "Who Qualifies as Métis?").

Why Is the *Manitoba Métis* Decision Important?

Métis – Honour of the Crown

The Supreme Court's 2013 Manitoba Métis *decision is important because it established that courts can make a declaration that the honour of the Crown has been breached regardless of how much time has passed since the wrong occurred.*

The Manitoba Act, which created Manitoba as a Canadian province in 1870, included a promise that 1.4 million acres of land would be set aside at Red River for the children of the Métis in exchange for the extinguishment of Métis Aboriginal title. Because this promise was not promptly fulfilled, the descendants of the Red River Métis were dispersed across the country. The Manitoba Métis Federation sued Canada for breach of fiduciary duty.

The Supreme Court decided Canada did not owe the Métis a fiduciary duty because Canada had not agreed to act in their best interests and because the Métis had not proven that historically there was a collective Métis interest in land. Instead, the evidence was that the Métis had bought and sold land as individuals. Without a collective interest in land, there could be no fiduciary duty. However, because the Manitoba Act is a constitutional document, the promise to set aside land for Métis children was a constitutional obligation. Canada's failure to diligently fulfill the obligation amounted to a breach of the honour of the Crown. The Métis were entitled to a court declaration that the honour of the Crown had been breached.

While the *Manitoba Métis* decision created a new avenue for Indigenous people to seek confirmation that the Crown has failed to fulfill its promises, its effectiveness remains in doubt. Following a declaration of a breach of the honour of the Crown, the expectation is the Crown will negotiate a just outcome. But, as the Court admitted at the time, the declaration does not require the Crown to do anything specific and may well be of no real consequence.

Why Is the *Daniels* Decision Important?

Métis – Section 91(24) – "Indians"

The Supreme Court's 2016 Daniels decision is important because it clarified that the federal government has law-making power over Métis and non-status Indians.

The constitution divides the Crown's law-making powers between the federal and provincial governments. Provinces make laws on various local and private matters including creating municipalities, establishing hospitals and managing public lands. The federal government legislates on matters of national importance including the postal service, banking and national defence (see "Why Is the Division of Powers Important?"). One of the topics on the federal side of the ledger is "Indians, and lands reserved for the Indians" in section 91(24) of the constitution. In 1939 the Court had decided "Indians" in section 91(24) includes the Inuit. The question in *Daniels* was whether it also includes Métis and non-status Indians.

The issue arose because the federal and provincial governments couldn't agree on which level of government was responsible for providing programs and services to Métis and non-status Indians. Frustrated with the stalemate, the Métis and non-status Indians sought clarification from the courts. At the Supreme Court, the federal government admitted "Indians" in section 91(24) includes non-status Indians. The remaining question for the Court was whether it also includes Métis.

The Court noted that historically it was widely accepted that "Indians" in section 91(24) included all Aboriginal people, including the Métis. This was because the federal government wanted to exercise jurisdiction over all Indigenous people in pursuit of its coast-to-coast colonization project. At various times, it had explicitly expanded its laws and policies aimed at "civilizing Indians" to include the Métis, including restrictions on the sale of liquor and forced attendance at residential schools.

While the Court decided "Indians" in section 91(24) includes the Métis, it rejected the argument that section 91(24) only includes people who can meet the test for Métis rights under section 35 of the constitution. The confusing result is that a person might be Métis and an Indian under section 91(24), but not qualify as either Métis or an Indian under section 35 of the constitution. Even more confusing, being an "Indian" under section 91(24) of the constitution does not mean a person is automatically an "Indian" under the Indian Act (see "Who is an Indian?"). *Daniels* confirms the federal government's authority to make laws that directly affect the Métis.

MISCELLANEOUS
AND EMERGING ISSUES

Why Is the BC Supreme Court's *Campbell* Decision Important?

Self-government – Indigenous Laws

The BC Supreme Court's 2000 Campbell decision is important because it recognized that Indigenous law-making authority pre-dated and existed separately from the Canadian constitution and was protected by section 35.

In 2000, after years of negotiation, Canada, British Columbia and the Nisga'a Nation entered into a treaty setting out the Nisga'a Nation's section 35 rights (see "Why Is the *Calder* Decision Important?"). The BC Liberal Party, which was in Opposition at the time, argued the treaty was invalid because it claimed to recognize Nisga'a law-making authority which, they said, didn't exist. The treaty identified a limited number of topics over which the Nisga'a would have exclusive law-making authority, e.g. Nisga'a identity, education and use of lands and resources. Should there be a conflict between these topics and federal or provincial laws, the Nisga'a laws prevail. For other topics, e.g. policing, if there's a conflict, federal or provincial laws prevail.

According to the BC Liberals, the Nisga'a couldn't exercise law-making authority under the treaty because Indigenous self-government rights were extinguished in 1867 when the Canadian constitution came into effect. They argued the constitution divided all law-making authority between the federal and provincial governments. The federal or provincial government might delegate law-making authority to a First Nation (e.g. through the Indian Act), but they couldn't give up their jurisdiction and there wasn't any inherent First Nation law-making authority.

The Court disagreed. It concluded that the Constitution Act, 1867 didn't intend to extinguish Indigenous self-government rights. It also didn't exhaust all law-making authority in Canada. Instead, it divided up the Crown's law-making authority between the federal and provincial governments. Indigenous law-making authority existed before the Constitution Act, 1867 and continued to exist afterwards. Since 1982, at least in respect to exercising decision-making over Aboriginal title land, it has been protected by section 35 of the constitution.

Although a lower court decision and nearly twenty-five years old, *Campbell* remains the clearest and most concise explanation in Canadian law of the legal basis for the inherent right of Indigenous Peoples to make their own laws.

Why Is the *Ross River Dena Council* Decision Important?

Reserve Creation

The Supreme Court's 2002 Ross River Dena Council decision is important because it established general requirements for creating Indian Act reserves.

Ross River Dena Council is an Indian Act band in Yukon. The band claimed the company it operated in its village was exempt from Yukon's taxation on tobacco sales because it was situated on Indian Act reserve land. Canada and Yukon disagreed. They claimed that despite the community having been located at the confluence of the Pelly and Ross Rivers since at least the 1950s, the land was not an Indian Act reserve. The Court agreed with Canada and Yukon.

Indian Act reserves are lands set apart for the use and benefit of an Indian Act band, but the act does not explain when and how lands are "set apart" and thus become reserve lands. While the process of reserve creation has varied widely across Canada, the Court identified basic requirements to create a reserve under the Indian Act: the Crown must take steps to set the land apart for the benefit of an Indian Act band, a Crown official with authority to bind the Crown must intend to set apart a reserve, and the band must accept the reserve and start using the land.

The Court decided that despite how often over the years the creation of a reserve for Ross River had been discussed, because a government official with authority to create an Indian Act reserve had never told Ross River the federal government was creating a reserve for them, an Indian Act reserve had never been legally created. The

Court suggested Ross River consider entering into a modern treaty in order to secure its village site.

The *Ross River* decision exemplifies the Court's willingness to abandon a liberal and generous application of the law, especially when land and taxation are at play and an alternative exists based on the surrender of Aboriginal title and rights.

Why Is the *Okanagan Indian Band* Decision Important?

Aboriginal Rights Litigation – Costs

The Supreme Court's 2003 Okanagan Indian Band decision is important because it established that in some cases it is justifiable to force governments to pay Indigenous Peoples' legal costs in advance of a court decision, and whether they win or lose.

In the fall of 1999, four British Columbia Indian Act bands (Adams Lake, Neskonlith, Okanagan and Spallumcheen) logged so-called Crown timber to build badly needed housing on their reserves. When they were charged by the provincial government, they raised a defence based on their Aboriginal title. Because of their desperate financial straits (they had a shortage of money for housing, education and basic infrastructure), they argued the court should order the Province to pay their legal bills in advance of a court decision and regardless of whether they won or lost.

The general rule is that the losing side pays a portion of the winning party's costs of the litigation. However, as early as 1742 the English courts recognized that in very exceptional cases a party with deep pockets might be ordered to make an advance payment to an impoverished party before the court made a decision to ensure that a case with merit wasn't abandoned for a lack of money.

The Court decided a judge can order one party to pay the opposing party's legal costs before a lawsuit is decided if three conditions are met. First, the party asking for the order genuinely can't afford to pay their legal costs and there is no other realistic option to fund the litigation. Second, on the face of it, their case has merit. Third, a decision in the case would be important to more than just the parties in court, i.e. the issues are important to the wider public and have not been decided yet by the courts.

The four First Nations met these requirements. They couldn't afford the cost of the litigation, their defence based on their Aboriginal title had merit and there had not yet been a court decision on the existence of Aboriginal title. The Court ordered the Province to pay their legal costs in advance of a decision in the case.

Unfortunately, the First Nations were unable to capitalize on their win at the Supreme Court because their case was later sidetracked on procedural grounds. It was the Tsilhqot'in Nation who benefitted the most. They used the same arguments to secure an advance cost order for their own Aboriginal title litigation. With sufficient funding, they proceeded to trial and ultimately the Supreme Court where they secured the first court declaration of Aboriginal title in Canadian history.

Why Is the BC Supreme Court's *Yahey* Decision Important?

Treaties – Infringement

The BC Supreme Court's 2021 Yahey decision is important because it was the first major court decision to consider cumulative effects of industrial development on treaty rights.

Blueberry River First Nations argued the British Columbia provincial government had authorized so much industrial development in its territory in northern BC that the cumulative effects amounted to an infringement of Treaty 8. The Province argued it could authorize the use of lands in Treaty 8 for various purposes, that it consulted about these authorizations and that it had not allowed so much land to be used for industrial purposes that Blueberry River had no meaningful ability to exercise treaty rights.

Most First Nation legal challenges focus on a single authorization that affects Aboriginal and treaty rights. *Yahey* was the first major court decision to consider the cumulative effects of multiple authorizations.

The Court emphasized Treaty 8 was not intended as a final agreement—it established the basis for an ongoing relationship. Treaty 8 included a fundamental promise that First Nations' way of life would be protected. While the Province could authorize various land uses, it had to ensure the Crown's Treaty 8 promises were respected and it couldn't significantly diminish First Nations' ability to exercise their treaty rights.

British Columbia had failed to uphold the Crown's treaty promises. Over many years it had allowed industrial development in Blueberry River's territory without assessing cumulative effects and without ensuring Blueberry River could meaningfully exercise its treaty rights (see "Why Is the *Mikisew I* Decision Important?").

Yahey is particularly important because the Court viewed the treaty as containing more than a bundle of harvesting rights. Instead, the fundamental treaty promise was that First Nations would be able to continue their way of life. The Province was responsible for diligently fulfilling this promise by implementing policies to monitor and address the cumulative effects of industrial development. Rather than appealing the decision, the Province chose to negotiate a resolution that addressed Blueberry River's and other Treaty 8 First Nations' concerns. The decision has inspired other treaty First Nations across Canada to file similar claims.

Why Is the BC Court of Appeal's *Saik'uz* Decision Important?

Aboriginal Rights – Nuisance – Companies

The BC Court of Appeal's 2024 Saik'uz decision is important because it confirmed First Nations can file claims against private companies for causing a nuisance that interferes with their Aboriginal rights.

Since the 1950s Saik'uz First Nation's and Stellat'en First Nation's fishing in the Nechako River, especially for white sturgeon and salmon, has been severely affected by Rio Tinto's operation of the Kenney Dam. The First Nations filed a lawsuit against the company for interfering with their Aboriginal fishing right and Aboriginal title.

The case, which started in 2011, raised several important issues that were decided at different times. In 2015 the BC Court of Appeal confirmed the First Nations could sue Rio Tinto, a private company, for causing a nuisance that affected their Aboriginal rights and title without having to first prove their rights existed. The Supreme Court rejected Rio Tinto's application to appeal the decision.

In 2022 the trial judge confirmed the First Nations' constitutional right to fish in the Nechako for food, social and ceremonial purposes and that the operation of the Kenney Dam significantly interfered with their fishing right. But, he decided as a matter of law Rio Tinto was not liable for causing a nuisance because its operations had been authorized by a provincial law.

In 2024, the BC Court of Appeal confirmed the company could rely on the provincial law that authorized the dam's operation as a defence against the nuisance claim, but that Canada and British Columbia must fulfill their fiduciary duty to the First Nations as part of their ongoing management of the Nechako River. This includes consulting the First Nations about any new adverse impacts on their fishing right.

Saik'uz, as well as a similar 2014 Quebec decision brought by the Innu, opened up the possibility of First Nations suing companies directly for activities that undermine their section 35 rights. Since the decisions, other First Nations across the country have filed similar lawsuits against companies. Assuming the companies weren't authorized by a federal or provincial law to interfere with the First Nations' rights, these lawsuits have a real chance of success.

Why Is the *Dickson* Decision Important?

Modern treaties – Charter of Rights

The Supreme Court's 2024 Dickson *decision is important because the Court decided the Canadian Charter of Rights and Freedoms applies to First Nations with self-government agreements, but that in some cases Charter rights will not be enforced because they interfere with Indigenous collective rights.*

Vuntut Gwitchin First Nation has a modern treaty and self-government agreement with Canada. Its constitution requires the elected Chief and Councillors to live on the First Nation's settlement lands about eight hundred kilometres north of Whitehorse, Yukon. Cindy Dickson, a member of the First Nation residing in Whitehorse, argued the residency requirement violated her Charter right to equality because it discriminated against her as a non-resident. The Court had to decide whether the Charter applied to the First Nation's constitution and if it did, whether Dickson's claim was defeated based on the need to protect the First Nation's treaty rights. In essence, the case was about individual rights versus collective rights.

In general, the Charter applies to the exercise of federal or provincial government authority. For this reason, it applies to Indian Act Chiefs and Councils because their authority is delegated from the federal government. In *Dickson*, the Court had to decide whether it also applied to self-governing First Nations. The judges disagreed. A majority of them decided the Charter applies to the Vuntut Gwitchin First Nation because whether or not it has inherent law-making authority, at least some of its authority is derived from the federal government's law-making authority over Indians and lands reserved for Indians under the constitution, i.e. section 91(24).

But there is also a section of the Charter that protects the collective Aboriginal and treaty rights, "or other rights or freedoms" of Aboriginal peoples from being abolished or undermined by the Charter, even when it's a First Nation member who brings the Charter challenge.

The majority of the judges understood the purposes of this protection as being the protection of Indigenous "difference," i.e. when there is a real conflict between an individual Charter right (e.g. equality) and a collective Indigenous right that can't be resolved, the latter would prevail if not doing so would undermine the difference between Indigenous Nations and mainstream Canada. They concluded that the residency requirement was an "other right," that Dickson's Charter claim couldn't be reconciled with it and therefore the First Nation's constitution prevailed.

Acknowledgements

This book wouldn't exist without the support of my colleagues at First Peoples Law LLP. I'm especially indebted to Kate Gunn with whom I've shared an ongoing conversation about Aboriginal law for well over a decade. Cody O'Neil's suggestions, corrections, edits and encouragement were invaluable in making this book much better than I could have done on my own.

As with all my writing, most of this book was written at the Café Calabria on Commercial Drive, Vancouver's oldest Italian coffee house. For over twenty-five years the Murdocco family has welcomed me early every morning with warmth, generosity and a perfectly made long black espresso.

I owe a debt of gratitude to Rolf Maurer at People's Co-op Bookstore on Commercial Drive for encouraging me to seek a publisher for my first book, *Standoff*, and to Silas White at Nightwood Editions for taking it on and for his careful and thoughtful editing of this volume.

Whether I start the day with writing, a meeting or a court appearance, it is the love and support of Emilie, Mojave, Phaedra and Tavish that sends me out into the world to do the work I'm honoured to do and brings me home at night.

When You Have More than One Minute

The brief summaries in this book no more than scratch the surface on complicated issues. The following reading suggestions are for those with both the time and inclination to dig deeper.

Indigenous Rights and Resistance

A good place to start is by reading Indigenous authors. The two books that were most influential in inspiring me to dedicate my professional life to the defence of Indigenous rights were Harold Cardinal's *The Unjust Society* (1969) and George Manuel and Michael Posluns's *The Fourth World* (1974). I also recommend Lee Maracle's *Bobbi Lee Indian Rebel* (1990).

For more recent books that carry on the tradition of Indigenous people speaking truth to power, you might start with Arthur Manuel and Grand Chief Ronald Derrickson's *Unsettling Canada* (2015) and *The Reconciliation Manifesto* (2017), Bev Sellars's *Price Paid* (2016) and Michelle Good's *Truth Telling* (2023). For an excellent essay collection on the Idle No More movement, check out *The Winter We Danced* (2014) edited by the Kino-nda-niimi Collective.

National Inquiries and Commissions

The following reports are fundamental to understanding Indigenous rights and Aboriginal law in Canada. They're all publicly available online.

Report of the Royal Commission on Aboriginal Peoples (1996).

Final Report of the Truth and Reconciliation Commission of Canada (2015).

Final Report of the National Inquiry into Missing and Murdered Indigenous Women and Girls (2019).

Indigenous Law

John Borrows's *Canada's Indigenous Constitution* (2010) is an excellent introduction to the topic of Indigenous legal traditions and their relationship to Canadian constitutional law.

There are also numerous examples of Indigenous Nations revitalizing and applying their laws to address pressing issues in their territories. A good example of this important work is the Tsleil-Waututh Nation's *Assessment of the Trans Mountain Pipeline and Tanker Expansion Proposal* (2015).

For more examples check out the valuable online resources created by the Indigenous Law Research Unit at the University of Victoria and the Wahkohtowin Law and Governance Lodge at the University of Alberta.

Aboriginal Law

Currently, the best primer on Aboriginal law, including foundational court cases, is Jim Reynolds's *Aboriginal Peoples and the Law* (2018).

Many academics have written books on Aboriginal law. The best of the lot is Michael Asch's *On Being Here to Stay* (2014), which provides a clear overview of Indigenous rights in Canadian law, especially treaty rights. It's also proof that legal analysis should never be the sole purview of lawyers.

For a readable primer on the Indian Act, check out Bob Joseph's *21 Things You May Not Know About the Indian Act* (2018), which justifiably continues to be a bestseller.

For those who want to dig deeper into the complexity and historical circumstances of important legal decisions, I recommend Kent McNeil's *Flawed Precedent* (2019) on the *St. Catherine's Milling* case, Jim Reynolds's *From Wardship to Rights* (2020) on the *Guerin* case, and *Let Right Be Done* (2008) on the *Calder* case edited by Hamar Foster, Heather Raven and Jeremy Webber.

Every year my colleagues at First Peoples Law LLP produce a new edition of *Indigenous Peoples and the Law in Canada*. It's invaluable for those looking for an up-to-date comprehensive resource summarizing court decisions and federal laws related to Indigenous Peoples.

UNDRIP

There is a lot of interest in how the United Nations Declaration on the Rights of Indigenous Peoples (UNDRIP) affects Indigenous people in Canada. While this issue continues to evolve at a rapid pace, as of the date of this publication the best starting point is the essay collection *Braiding Legal Orders* (2019) edited by John Borrows, Larry Chartrand, Oonagh E. Fitzgerald and Risa Schwartz.

You should also check out the online resources (including great video content) related to UNDRIP implementation in Canada created by the Yellowhead Institute and the Centre for International Governance Innovation at yellowheadinstitute.org and www.cigionline.org.

Sheryl Lightfoot's *Global Indigenous Politics* provides a helpful history and analysis of how UNDRIP came to be in the context of Indigenous Peoples' efforts to defend and advance their rights in the international arena.

Indigenous Rights News

For a weekly news update on Indigenous rights across the country, subscribe to the First Peoples Law Report at firstpeopleslaw.com. I started this weekly newsletter thirteen years ago by sending it out to about fifty clients and colleagues. We're now close to twenty thousand subscribers. You can also find succinct and accessible commentary of the top legal issues on our blog.

To keep up to date on Canada's reconciliation scorecard, including action (and inaction) on the Truth and Reconciliation Commission's Calls to Action, you'll want to bookmark Indigenous Watchdog at indigenouswatchdog.org.

For top-notch Indigenous policy perspectives, keep your eye out for the Yellowhead Institute's reports and other features at yellowhead institute.org.

Beyond the Law

Often the best entry point for understanding Indigenous rights in Canada is to read the work of contemporary Indigenous authors. A good place to start is to unlearn the standard history most Canadians are taught in high school. Two recent books that will be an eye-opener for many Canadians are Tanya Talaga's *The Knowing* (2024) and Jody Wilson-Raybould and Roshan Danesh's *Reconciling History: A Story of Canada* (2024).

When the language of the law fails, which it often does, I find clarity, empathy and understanding in the creative writing of Indigenous people. To choose just a few from a long list of important works, you will not go wrong by picking up Tanya Tagaq's *Split Tooth* (2018), Joshua Whitehead's essay collection *Making Love with the Land* (2022) and Billy-Ray Belcourt's short story collection *Coexistence* (2024). Jordan Abel's *Empty Spaces* (2024) was a well-deserved winner of the Governor General's Literary Award for Fiction, but many might prefer to enjoy it by listening to Elle-Máijá Tailfeathers's hauntingly beautiful audiobook narration. A perfect companion to Abel's book is Jess Housty's award-winning collection of poetry, *Crushed Wild Mint* (2023). And for those with young children, I recommend Samantha Beynon and Lucy Trimble's beautiful *Oolichan Moon* (2022).

Other Resources

If you prefer podcasts, videos and other media, check out First Peoples Law's multimedia list at www.firstpeopleslaw.com/public-education/reading-lists.

The Top 50 Aboriginal Law Court Decisions

Anderson v. Alberta, 2022 SCC 6

Beckman v. Little Salmon/Carmacks First Nation, 2010 SCC 53, [2010] 3 S.C.R. 103

Behn v. Moulton Contracting Ltd., 2013 SCC 26, [2013] 2 S.C.R. 227

British Columbia (Minister of Forests) v. Okanagan Indian Band, [2003] 3 S.C.R. 371, 2003 SCC 71

Calder et al. v. Attorney-General of British Columbia, [1973] S.C.R. 313

Campbell et al v. AG BC/AG Cda & Nisga'a Nation et al, 2000 BCSC 1123

Chippewas of the Thames First Nation v. Enbridge Pipelines Inc., 2017 SCC 41, [2017] 1 S.C.R. 1099

Clyde River (Hamlet) v. Petroleum Geo-Services Inc., 2017 SCC 40, [2017] 1 S.C.R. 1069

Daniels v. Canada (Indian Affairs and Northern Development), 2016 SCC 12, [2016] 1 S.C.R. 99

Delgamuukw v. British Columbia, [1997] 3 S.C.R. 1010

Dickson v. Vuntut Gwitchin First Nation, 2024 SCC 10

Grassy Narrows First Nation v. Ontario (Natural Resources), 2014 SCC 48, [2014] 2 S.C.R. 447

Guerin v. The Queen, [1984] 2 S.C.R. 335

Haida Nation v. British Columbia (Minister of Forests), [2004] 3 S.C.R. 511, 2004 SCC 73

Manitoba Metis Federation Inc. v. Canada (Attorney General), 2013 SCC 14, [2013] 1 S.C.R. 623

Mikisew Cree First Nation v. Canada (Governor General in Council), 2018 SCC 40, [2018] 2 S.C.R. 765

Mikisew Cree First Nation v. Canada (Minister of Canadian Heritage), [2005] 3 S.C.R. 388, 2005 SCC 69

Mitchell v. M.N.R., [2001] 1 S.C.R. 911, 2001 SCC 33

Nowegijick v. The Queen, [1983] 1 S.C.R. 29

Ontario (Attorney General) v. Restoule, 2024 SCC 27

Osoyoos Indian Band v. Oliver (Town), [2001] 3 S.C.R. 746, 2001 SCC 85

Reference re An Act respecting First Nations, Inuit and Métis children, youth and families, 2024 SCC 5

Rio Tinto Alcan Inc. v. Carrier Sekani Tribal Council, 2010 SCC 43, [2010] 2 S.C.R. 650

Ross River Dena Council Band v. Canada, [2002] 2 S.C.R. 816, 2002 SCC 54

R. v. Adams, [1996] 3 S.C.R. 101

R. v. Badger, [1996] 1 S.C.R. 771

R. v. Côté, [1996] 3 S.C.R. 139

R. v. Desautel, 2021 SCC 17, [2021] 1 S.C.R. 533

R. v. Gladstone, [1996] 2 S.C.R. 723

R. v. Horseman, [1990] 1 S.C.R. 901

R. v. Marshall, [1999] 3 S.C.R. 456

R. v. Marshall, [1999] 3 S.C.R. 533

R. v. Nikal, [1996] 1 S.C.R. 1013

R. v. N.T.C. Smokehouse Ltd., [1996] 2 S.C.R. 672

R. v. Pamajewon, [1996] 2 S.C.R. 821

R. v. Powley, [2003] 2 S.C.R. 207, 2003 SCC 43

R. v. Sioui, [1990] 1 S.C.R. 1025

R. v. Sparrow, [1990] 1 S.C.R. 1075

R. v. Sundown, [1999] 1 S.C.R. 393

R. v. Van der Peet, [1996] 2 S.C.R. 507

Shot Both Sides v. Canada, 2024 SCC 12

Simon v. The Queen, [1985] 2 S.C.R. 387

Southwind v. Canada, 2021 SCC 28, [2021] 2 S.C.R. 450

St. Catharines Milling and Lumber Co. v. R, (1887) 13 S.C.R. 577

Taku River Tlingit First Nation v. British Columbia (Project Assessment Director), [2004] 3 S.C.R. 550, 2004 SCC 74

Thomas and Saik'uz First Nation v. Rio Tinto Alcan Inc., 2022 BCSC 15

Tsilhqot'in Nation v. British Columbia, 2014 SCC 44, [2014] 2 S.C.R. 256

Wewaykum Indian Band v. Canada, [2003] 2 S.C.R. 259, 2003 SCC 45

Williams Lake Indian Band v. Canada (Aboriginal Affairs and Northern Development), 2018 SCC 4, [2018] 1 S.C.R. 83

Yahey v British Columbia, 2021 BCSC 1287

Glossary

Many of these terms have complicated legal meanings. I've simplified the following explanations to make them accessible to non-lawyers. For more precision and legal nuance, consult *Indigenous Peoples and the Law in Canada*, a yearly publication written by my colleagues at First Peoples Law. *Native Law* by Jack Woodward and *Constitutional Law of Canada* by Peter Hogg are also valuable starting points.

Aboriginal People of Canada: a group of Indigenous people whose collective rights are protected under section 35 of the constitution.

Adams **point**: a legal principle derived from the Supreme Court's *Adams* decision. It holds that if a law allows a government decision-maker to decide whether or not Indigenous people can exercise an Aboriginal right, the law must include specific criteria they need to follow when making their decision. The absence of criteria can in itself be an infringement of the Aboriginal right.

asserted rights: Aboriginal rights protected by section 35, but which have not been recognized by the courts or the Crown; i.e., they are denied.

assertion of Crown sovereignty: a political act by which the British Crown asserted ultimate law-making authority over Indigenous lands and Indigenous people; i.e., a Canadian euphemism for the Doctrine of Discovery. The date of the assertion of Crown sovereignty differs across the country based on historical circumstances.

cede, release and surrender: a phrase found in many historical treaties. The Crown usually takes the position that it represents a Treaty nation's agreement to surrender its land—Indigenous people disagree. It was most likely not explained to the Indigenous people who agreed to the treaty and if it was, they most likely did not understand its legal effect under Canadian law. The Crown uses different language in modern treaties but maintains that the effect of the treaty is basically the same.

cognizable interest: a principle from fiduciary law, it is an interest capable of being recognized under Canadian law; e.g., a First Nation's interest in its Indian Act reserve lands.

constitutional democracy: a democratic country with a constitution as its highest law. If a legislature (i.e., parliament or a provincial legislature) passes a law contrary to the constitution, the courts must strike it down.

cumulative effects: the combined effects on section 35 rights of numerous provincial or federal government authorizations; e.g., roads, logging, hydro-dams, transmission lines, mining, etc.

de facto control: the Crown's control of Indigenous lands as a matter of fact, but not based on a recognized legal right. The Supreme Court famously commented on the difference in the 2004 *Haida* decision in reference to so-called Crown land in British Columbia.

discretionary control: a principle from fiduciary law often required to establish whether the Crown owed Indigenous people a fiduciary duty. It's based on the Crown assuming control of an Indigenous legal interest recognized under Canadian law; e.g., a First Nation's interest in its Indian Act reserve lands.

Doctrine of Discovery: a legal principle developed by the United States Supreme Court in the 1820s and 1830s based on the racist principle that by simply "discovering" Indigenous lands European colonizers acquired an interest in those lands and displaced Indigenous Peoples' law-making authority.

duty to consult and accommodate: the Crown's constitutional obligation to consult, and perhaps accommodate, Indigenous people whenever it proposes making a decision that might affect section 35 rights.

fiduciary duty: a legal obligation to act in someone else's best interests (e.g., a Crown fiduciary duty to a First Nation) which is enforceable in court.

honour of the Crown: a constitutional principle that governments must always deal fairly and honourably with Indigenous people.

Indian Act band: a group of status Indians with a collective interest in land or other property that is controlled by the federal government; e.g., reserve land or a trust account.

Indigenous Nation: most often used to refer to an Indigenous, self-governing nation that predated the arrival of European colonizers. In this sense, it is equivalent to the term "Nations or Tribes of Indians" used by the British in the Royal Proclamation of 1763.

Land Back: a movement which recognizes Indigenous Peoples' inherent authority over their lands.

non-status Indian: a person who identifies as a member of an Indian Act band, i.e. a First Nation, but is not entitled to be a registered member under the Indian Act.

non-treaty First Nation: an Indigenous Nation or Indian Act band without a historical or modern treaty with the Crown. Because their section 35 constitutional rights may not be recognized by the federal and provincial governments, they often rely on the United Nations Declaration on the Rights of Indigenous Peoples and the duty to consult and accommodate to protect their rights.

no-veto principle: a principle in Canadian law that holds that while the Crown may have a legal obligation to consult and accommodate Indigenous people, in most cases it does not need Indigenous people's agreement. It's often misapplied to support pushing through a Crown decision over Indigenous people's objections.

Nowegijick **principle**: a general principle derived from the Supreme Court's *Nowegijick* decision. It holds that when interpreting laws relating to Indigenous people, including the Indian Act, any uncertainty should be interpreted in favour of Indigenous people.

parliamentary sovereignty: the legal principle that a legislature (e.g., the federal parliament or a provincial legislature) has the power to make any law or abolish any existing law as long as it adheres to the constitution.

Powley **test**: the three general requirements for identifying Métis under section 35 set down by the Supreme Court in the 2003 *Powley* decision: self-identification, ancestral connection and community acceptance.

procedural aspects of consultation: the parts of the consultation process the Crown can assign to someone else, e.g. companies. This includes sharing information, answering questions and discussing possible mitigation measures. It is to be contrasted with the substantive aspects of the duty to consult the Crown cannot assign to someone else; e.g., accommodating Indigenous Peoples' decision-making authority.

procedural right: the right to a process, but not to any particular outcome. The duty to consult and accommodate is a procedural right, i.e. Indigenous people have a right to a process based on principles set down by the courts, but they do not have a right to any specific outcome. In contrast, recognized rights are substantive rights; e.g., infringing Aboriginal title would require real, concrete compensation.

recognized rights: section 35 rights recognized under a historical or modern treaty or by way of a court decision. They might also be recognized by governments without a treaty but the courts will make the final decision on whether they are section 35 rights.

Royal Proclamation of 1763: a proclamation made by King George III at the end of the Seven Years' War between Britain and France that drew a north-south line between the American thirteen colonies and lands to the west. Through it the British Crown asserted sovereignty over Indigenous Peoples' lands while also recognizing inherent rights.

scope of the duty to consult: the consultation obligations owed to Indigenous people once the duty is triggered. The scope of the duty to consult exists on a spectrum from minimal to much more onerous obligations. The scope is determined by the potential impact of the Crown decision plus the importance of the section 35 right.

section 91(24): a section in the Canadian constitution that assigns to the federal government, versus the provincial governments, exclusive law-making authority for "Indians, and lands reserved for the Indians." In practice, the courts have upheld the application of many provincial laws to "Indians, and lands reserved for the Indians" and only enforce the federal government's exclusive law-making authority for laws that directly affect what the courts have described as the "core of Indianness"; e.g., Indian Act reserve lands, child and family services, etc.

section 35 Indian: a person entitled to exercise Aboriginal rights under section 35 of the constitution because they are a member of one of the Aboriginal Peoples of Canada. They do not have to be a status Indian or a Canadian citizen.

section 91(24) Indian: includes status Indians, non-status Indians, Métis and Inuit. As between the federal and provincial governments, the federal government has the exclusive authority to pass laws that directly affect them. These people do not necessarily have rights under section 35 of the constitution.

status Indian: a person registered or entitled to be registered as an Indian under the Indian Act.

treaty First Nation: an Indigenous Nation or Indian Act band with a historical or modern treaty with the Crown. Their treaty rights are recognized under section 35 of the constitution but can be infringed if the Crown follows the requirements set down by the Supreme Court.

trigger for the duty to consult: a Crown action with sufficient potential to affect a section 35 right that the Crown must consult Indigenous people. The threshold for triggering the duty to consult is minimal.

Index I: General

Index II: Court Decisions

About the Author

PHOTO CREDIT: KATHRYN LANGSFORD

Originally from Manitoba's Interlake region, Bruce McIvor lives and works in Vancouver. He is founder and senior partner at First Peoples Law LLP and an adjunct professor at the University of British Columbia's Allard School of Law. His work includes both litigation and negotiation on behalf of Indigenous Peoples across Canada. Bruce is recognized nationally and internationally as a leading practitioner of Aboriginal law in Canada. His collection of essays entitled *Standoff: Why Reconciliation Fails Indigenous People and How to Fix It* was published in the fall of 2021. Bruce is a member of the Manitoba Métis Federation. He is currently working on new creative writing projects that explore the intersection of law, history and Indigenous rights. For updates on his writing, go to www.brucemcivor.com or email him at bruce@brucemcivor.com.